Crime Fiction and the Indie Contribution

Chris Longmuir

B&J

ISBN: 978-1499325249

This book is dedicated to all those indie authors and publishers who are publishing quality books for discerning readers.

CONTENTS

1

Introduction

The idea for this book came from some blog posts I wrote for an online book festival. I was approached by the organizer and asked if I would submit a series of articles on crime fiction. The festival planned to run for fourteen days, and my remit was to supply twelve items on crime topics.

After some thought I decided to base the twelve articles on the subgenres of crime fiction, ranging from mystery and cosy, through to noir. Initially, I thought I could use books I had previously read to illustrate these articles, but on further examination of my task I realized that this would not be appropriate.

Electronic books are fairly new on the scene, a few years at most, which meant the bulk of my lifetime of reading had been provided by traditional authors with traditional publishing deals. This was a problem because the online festival is all about electronic books, and this dictated that all my reading choices had to be e-books. Moreover, because the festival promotes indie authors, the name by which the new breed of independently publishing writers have become known, those e-books had to be written by indie authors, or be published by indie publishers.

I embarked on the research with enthusiasm because I have been reading crime fiction most of my adult life, as well as more recently writing it. My resources were mainly secondary ones. I consulted studies on crime fiction, reference books on the subject, and ones which took a wider view of all genres of fiction. And, of course, this being research into the independent world of e-books, material sourced on the internet had to be included. Finally, I read a wide range of indie crime fiction to illustrate the subgenres I was writing about.

I wrote twelve blog posts in total, and in each of those posts I considered three books from the indie range of crime authors. It took me a good six months to read all the books I featured in my posts, plus a few more novels which were scrapped as not measuring up to the standard I was looking for. This amounted to a formidable number of books. Nothing daunted, I made my list of books to fit the categories I intended to discuss, and buckled down to it, writing each blog post as soon as I had finished each section on my list. The posts were subsequently featured on the festival pages where they were well received and widely read. This confirmed to me that there was considerable interest in the subject.

The online festival which was the Edinburgh e-Book Festival – not the traditional book festival in Edinburgh – but one which ran alongside it and catered for a worldwide electronic community who had no access to the physical festival. All that was needed to take part was access to a wireless connection and the internet, as well as an electronic device, for example, a computer, smartphone, or a tablet computer such as the iPad.

The first ever Edinburgh e-Book Festival was held in 2012, and is scheduled to be repeated on an annual basis every August. The festival features the indie writers and publishers of e-books. A programme of events is scheduled for set times during the day over a 14 day period which runs at the same time as the official Edinburgh Book Festival. But where the official festival is concerned with traditionally published print books, the online festival, by its very nature, is digital and was originally text based. The digital world is expanding, however, and the festival now has video input, as well as interactive workshops. I anticipate it will continue to expand, and thought has already been given to Skype and video conferencing. The festival is organized and run by Cally Phillips, and in her words, *"e-books are consumed digitally, so why not have a digital festival for e-books."*

The articles I wrote for the festival generated a great deal of interest, but following the closure of the 2013 festival the information was removed from the site. I have been contacted by many people who still wanted to read the original blog posts, and this is the main reason I decided to incorporate them into book form.

The task has been greater than I anticipated because it has meant expanding and rewriting the original blog posts in a style more suited to book form. I have also incorporated a short history of crime fiction, as well as more information in connection with e-books, publishing options, and the emergence of the indie author. Additional categories of crime fiction have been added and a more in depth look at all the subgenres.

Over the course of this book I will look at indie crime fiction and attempt to assess how it compares with traditionally published books. I will try to give some guidance to readers in an area of publishing which is expanding at a phenomenal rate. It is my hope that by doing so I will encourage readers to experiment with their choice of authors and books.

2

E-books and E-readers – What are they?

E-books and E-readers

Before I go on to discuss indie writers and their contribution to crime fiction, I thought it would be useful to talk about e-books and e-readers.

In many readers' eyes, e-books belong to the technological age. They are not like the books they have been accustomed to in the past, and are considered to be a new development. Some readers have embraced the new ways of reading, others are convinced that nothing can replace print books.

In simple terms, the e-book is a digital or electronic book. It is a file that is computer generated and is read on a computer screen or a hand held device such as an e-reader. There is an unfortunate spin off from this because the reader who buys the e-book may not see it as a product requiring payment. A paper book is a physical thing as is the e-reader to which the e-book is downloaded, but the e-book can appear to be simply words that appear on the e-reader. As a result many readers expect all e-books to be free in the same way many internet downloads are free.

However, the publication of the e-book file does have a cost. The writer has spent time writing the words contained within the file, and it may have taken a year or longer to complete a book or novel. It also has the normal start up costs that print books have; for example, payment for the cover art, the illustrator, the editor, and the formatting. The advantage an e-book has over a print book is the saving on printing, storage and distribution costs. This is the reason e-books can be sold at a cheaper price than a comparable print book.

A print book can be bought from a bookstore, a supermarket, or the internet, from a variety of stores such as Amazon, Barnes and Noble, and Waterstones. An e-book requires to be downloaded from an online store including the ones already mentioned. To read the e-book it requires a screen which can be a computer screen, a tablet such as the iPad, or a dedicated e-reader.

An e-reader is designed specifically for the purpose of reading digital e-books and publications. It is a mobile electronic device much the same size and shape as a physical print book. The advantage it has over the print book is its portability. It is lighter than a print book and can contain many thousands of books which are available to read at the touch of a button. Many models have wireless connectivity, with a direct link to an online e-bookstore, which means an e-book can be bought at any time and be immediately available. There is no need to wait for a bookstore to open, or make the journey to buy a book. It is ideal for travellers, although many readers now prefer their electronic e-reader to a print book, to be read at any time. Others read both.

Another advantage e-books and e-readers have is the ability to adjust the size of text, something you cannot do with a print book. This is helpful for those readers whose vision is not perfect. Likewise, the e-reader is easier to hold than a print book because it does not require pages to be held open.

There are different makes of e-reader and they do not all use the same type of files, although most e-books are published in every file format. However, what can be read on one make of e-reader may not necessarily be readable on another. For example, Amazon's Kindle uses its own file format based on mobi files. Many other e-readers use the epub format which is readable on e-readers using the same format. The exception is the Barnes and Noble Nook which uses a different version of epub file. Then there is DRM (Digital Rights Management) which encrypts e-books so they can only be read on the device belonging to the buyer. Some e-book sellers insist the e-books they sell are DRM protected, others do not. Amazon, for example, makes DRM encryption optional for Kindle e-books. To ensure an e-book is compatible with a specific e-reader the buyer would be advised to use the store associated with their e-reader, although more knowledgeable buyers have the ability to shop around.

E-readers continue to develop, and some of the latest models have more resemblance to tablet computers. These include the Apple iPad, the Kindle Fire, and various android tablets. The difference between them and the original e-reader is the screen. The dedicated e-readers, such as Amazon's Kindle (not the Kindle Fire), Barnes and Noble's Nook, W H Smith's Kobo, and the Sony Reader, use an electronic paper technology called e-ink. Reading from screens using this type of display is easier on the eye; the text is displayed as black print on a white or cream background which makes it similar to reading a printed page. There is no glare on the screen from sunlight and, similar to a print book, the e-book can be read in any lighting condition apart from the dark. The newer tablet models have full colour, they can be used for other activities as well as reading, such as games, music, video, emails, and browsing the internet. However, the screens are reflective and they do not use an e-ink display. The outcome is that they are less easy on the eye, and are impossible to read in sunlight.

History of E-books and E-readers
The rapid increase in the sales of e-books and e-readers over the

past few years gives the impression that this technology is new and is a twenty-first century development. Nothing could be further from the truth.

Project Gutenberg was launched in 1971. This was the year they digitized the *United States Declaration of Independence,* making it the first e-book in the world. The aim of this voluntary project is to digitize all books which are no longer in copyright in order to preserve them for future generations. Volunteers retype and scan the out-of-copyright texts. Books by Jane Austen, Charlotte Bronte, Sir Arthur Conan Doyle, H G Wells, and a host of others can be found on the Project Gutenberg web site for free download. And from a small start with one book in 1971 the project has grown and now contains over 42,000 free books, most of them classics.

However, it was the 1990s before the development of e-book publication started to progress. In 1991 the Project Gutenberg began to take its present form, and the target at that time was to digitize one book each month. By 1996 it was a book a day, and today about 400 books are added each month. Then in 1993, Digital Book Inc. produced the first fifty digital books on floppy disc.

The way in which people read e-books has also progressed over the years. In the early days e-books were read on computers, and software was produced to enable the e-book to be read in a similar fashion to a traditional book. The most popular reader software at the time was the Adobe Reader, originally known as Adobe Acrobat Reader, launched in 1993, and Microsoft Reader, in 2000. Both these computer based readers are still available, and Adobe Reader is widely used to read PDF (portable document format) files, although Microsoft Reader is not so popular. An early e-book was a Stephen King novella, *Riding the Bullet,* which was published in 2000 in digital form to be read on a computer. I have been unable to determine which reader software the e-book used but I suspect it was Microsoft Reader which was launched in the same year the novella was published. It is estimated that 400,000 copies were downloaded in the first hour causing many computers to crash.

A variety of portable devices were appearing on the market as early as 1998, when the Rocket E-book and the Softbook were launched. These were the predecessors of the e-readers available today, but their capacity was far less. Instead of the thousands of e-books the modern versions can hold, these early e-readers struggled to contain 10 books. Over the years e-readers continued to develop culminating in the ones we have today.

The Sony Reader was the first to be launched in Britain in 2008, although it had been on sale in the US since 2006. This was followed soon after by Amazon's Kindle in 2007 in the US, although it was not available in the UK until 2009. Other popular e-readers were slower to appear in the UK, with W H Smith introducing the Kobo Reader in their stores in 2011, while Barnes and Noble introduced their Nook reader to the UK in 2012.

E-books versus Print Books

E-books and e-readers have gained popularity over the last few years and, while many readers will not forsake the printed book, the numbers reading e-books have increased substantially.

Statistics indicate that, in the US, the revenue from sales of e-books grew from $64 million to $3,042 million between 2008 to 2012, and the number of actual e-books sold increased from 10 million to 457 million over the same period. That is a massive increase. However, it does not tell the full story because the statistics are compiled by the AAP (Association of American Publishers) and the figures are obtained through

Bowker, the ISBN book registering agency. Many indie e-books are not registered with an ISBN because e-books sold by Amazon for the Kindle do not require one. Therefore, it is logical to assume that the figures are grossly underestimated and the sales of e-books are far greater.

The following statistics originated from Amazon in relation to Kindle Direct Publishing which is where indie authors publish their e-books: *"more than a thousand KDP authors now each sell more than a thousand copies a month, some have already reached hundreds of thousands of sales, and two have already joined the Kindle Million Club."*

The Million Club is for authors who have sold a million e-books. There are only fourteen authors in this club to date, and the two indie authors who qualify for the Million Club are John Locke and Amanda Hocking. The others are bestselling authors Lee Child, Nora Roberts, George R R Martin, Charlaine Harris, James Patterson, Janet Evanovich, Stieg Larsson, Michael Connolly, David Baldacci, Suzanne Colins, Kathryn Stockett, and Stephanie Meyer.

To have obtained such a large share of the book buying market over a relatively short time indicates that e-books are providing a satisfying reading experience for readers. The number of sales indicated by the indie author publishing platform KDP (Kindle Direct Publishing) confirms my belief that there are many quality indie e-books available.

The Indie E-book
It is said that one of the advantages of e-publishing is that 'anyone can publish a book,' and one of the disadvantages is that 'anyone can publish a book.' I think this illustrates the current e-publishing situation. There are many well written, well edited and formatted e-books available, but likewise, the reverse

can be true.

There is no excuse for badly written, and badly edited books, although formatting comes into a different category. Some well written books are let down by bad formatting, however, this is not exclusive to indie e-books. Many traditionally published e-books suffer from formatting glitches as well. I think that may be due to some publishers using their print files to publish e-books. When publishing a print book the format used is PDF (portable document format), this is a fixed format, once the print is placed on the page it does not move. E-books, however, require a format which makes the the print flow from line to line in accordance with the size of the font in order to maintain the readability of the page on a screen.

Apart from this, a book that is perfectly laid out may inexplicably develop irregularities in the formatting due to the conversion process. This can replace symbols for certain letters, particularly noticeable in traditionally published books where the conversions have been made using layouts for hardbacks and paperbacks.

The indie e-book is perhaps less prone to this type of formatting glitch because indie books generally appear as e-books first, and the formatting is specific to electronic publishing. Nevertheless, the conversion process can still throw up errors.

It is for this reason, that in my study of indie crime fiction, I will not allow minor formatting glitches to influence my opinion of a book, although if there are major glitches resulting from carelessness rather than the conversion process, this will result in a less favourable report.

3
What is an Indie?

The Indie

Indie is short for independent. Indie authors are writers who are bypassing traditional publishers and are publishing their books independently. They are responsible for everything, from the initial writing through to the sale of the finished product. The indie author, by default, also becomes an indie publisher, although the indie label also applies to small independent publishers with one or more authors on their books. The books produced by the indie author or publisher are not part of main stream publishing by major companies whose names are household words. You know the ones I mean, Penguin, Harper Collins, Macmillan, and the others.

The name 'indie' was not coined by self-publishing authors, it has earlier connections with the music industry and with films. But it has the same meaning, something that is independently produced. I am not aware of when it started to be used for books and literature which were previously referred to as self-published, but the name seems appropriate, and it works to prevent confusion between the independent self-publishing author and vanity publishing.

I have looked at various definitions of indie, and it always comes back to something produced by an independent artist, studio, producer, writer, company, or group, which is not affiliated with a larger or more commercial organisation. In the case of literature it is a book published outside of mainstream publishing.

In an article, at CNN.com (Cable News Network), journalist Catherine Andrews wrote: *"The term 'indie' traditionally refers to independent art – music, film, literature or anything that fits under the broad banner of culture – created outside of the mainstream and without corporate financing."*

So, indie authors are writers who self-publish their books. But don't let that put you off reading them because many indie books on sale are excellent. I admit, however, there are some that should never have been published, but it is relatively easy to separate those from the well written ones. If you do make a mistake and pick up one of the latter they are so cheap it is not a great loss. And there are ways of checking the quality of an e-book such as the 'Look Inside' and the 'Try a Sample' features on Amazon.

But I am sure you are wondering why a writer would choose to be an indie? Why go through all the hassle of independently publishing your book when there may be publishers ready and willing to publish it for you? Before I tackle that issue, perhaps you would like to see what options an author has to attain publication.

Publishing Options
The author has completed the book, has had it edited and proof read, it is as good as it can be, and it is ready for publication. What are the options?

1. Traditional Publisher
The traditional or legacy publisher is often the first choice. How hard can it be? The author who chooses to follow this route starts off on a merry-go-round of submissions and rejections. Time is taken out to look for an agent which leads to more submissions and rejections. You may think this only applies to

new authors, those who have never published before, but I am afraid it is exactly the same for authors with a track record who are not currently under contract to a publisher. Representation by an agent is probably the only advantage the professional author may have over the new author. The outcome, however, is often the same. This is because publishers are in business to sell books, and the publication of a book is simply a means to the end. That is why you see so many celebrity biographies and cook books on the bookstore shelves. However, if the publisher thinks your book will sell in the millions then you may get that elusive contract, although a friend of mine in the publishing industry informed me most first novels sell less than 300 copies.

In financial terms royalties are paid at the rate of anything between 7.5% to 10% for paperbacks. Many publishers give the author an advance payment, but this is an advance of royalties, it is not a payment for writing the book. If, for example, £1,000 is given before publication of the book no royalties will be paid until they exceed the amount of the advance.

2. Small Press

If the author has been unable to interest a traditional publisher there are always the small presses, the small publishers, and the independents. The chances of acceptance may be greater here, but small presses and publishers have small budgets to match, so may be restricted in what they can take on. Small publishers rarely pay royalty advances, and I have noticed some of them price their books higher than their bigger brothers, the traditional publishers, which makes their books less competitive in a crowded market.

Small presses often use the same service suppliers and distributors as the self-publishers. The main benefit for the author, if they publish this way, is they do not have to do everything themselves. However, marketing and distribution may be less than that provided by a larger publishing house. The new author also needs to be aware that a major disadvantage when seeking publication by a small press is the number of vanity publishers masquerading as small publishers. Unlike the traditional and small press publishers, the vanity publisher will expect the author to pay a fee for publication. This makes it essential for the author to research a small press before signing a contract.

3. *Self-publish*

Self-publishing has had a bad press over the years and there is still a stigma attached to it, although that is gradually lessening. It is important to remember that this method of publishing includes the vanity publishers as well as the indies. A vanity publisher will promise everything and will charge accordingly. They are in the business of selling publishing services to authors. They are unconcerned about the content or quality of the writing and will promise to distribute the books after they are published, but in most cases do not do this. The only person they distribute to is the author.

With self-publishing the author pays the expenses for editing, cover art, and formatting. There should be no fee attached to publication. If there is, then the chances are the author has fallen foul of a vanity publisher.

There are various ways to self-publish. For example, Amazon's CreateSpace, FeedaRead, and Lulu.com, are reputable self-publishing firms who use print on demand, and I am sure there are others, but care should be taken to ensure they are not vanity publishers.

4. *Print on Demand (POD)*

This is a better way to publish books than using a vanity press. The costs involved are the print costs, and if dealing with a local printer these can be negotiated. Of course, there is more work involved in formatting, providing a book cover etc, but this work can be outsourced if necessary. With POD each copy of a book costs more than copies supplied by a large print run, but although a print run can be cheaper there is the temptation to order too many copies to keep the price down, and this can lead to storage problems and unsold books.

5. Electronic
Publishing an e-book is relatively simple; it is cost free if everything is done by the author. However, it is better to outsource the editing and proofreading, and the book cover. The formatting can also be outsourced if the author is technologically challenged, although it is comparatively easy to do with a modicum of time and patience. Once initial expenses are accounted for there is no further outlay. Financially, royalties for the self-publishing indie author range between 35% to 85%, depending on the distributor and the price of the book. By comparison, mainstream publishers pay anything between 17.5% and 20% royalties to the traditionally published author when they publish their books as e-books.

Reasons Why Authors Choose to Publish Independently
The answer is, of course, in the heading. The main reason an author becomes an indie is because it makes them truly independent. They make their own decisions and pay all the bills associated with publishing their books. However, authors may take various routes to get there before they make a final decision. So, perhaps it would be helpful to look at some of the things that can affect their decision.

1. The author is tired of being knocked back by publishers and agents, and tired of the constant rejections, so they decide to go it alone.

Many people associate this with failure, and the self-publishing stigma can kick in labelling the authors as 'wannabes' who have been unable to attain success elsewhere. This is doing a great disservice to the writers involved, although there may be some among them who deserve this label. The majority, however, do not. It is worth bearing in mind that these writers are not all newbies. Many of them are professional authors with a wealth of experience, and have previously published using traditional means.

2. Lost contracts.

Due to the changing publishing scene and the economic climate, many mid-list authors are losing their contracts. Some of these authors have published regularly, year after year, for their publisher, and now find themselves no longer wanted. They may try to get a foothold in the publishing industry with another publisher, but only a few succeed.

3. The backlist.

Prolific authors with many published books now out of print, and where the publishing rights have reverted to the author, are giving their books a new lease of life as e-books.

4. Making money.

Some writers, especially the ones new to publishing, become indie authors and publishers because they believe all authors make oodles of money. They read the media releases about indie writers striking it big and making millions. They read about *Fifty Shades of Grey*, and authors such as John Locke, and Amanda Hocking, and think it is easy. However, the sad truth is writers and authors in general do not make a lot of money, and the majority do not make a living wage.

5. They want to attract a publisher.

Stories abound, particularly on the internet, that the big publishers are using indie books as their new slush pile, and are cherry picking authors who appear to be selling an inordinate number of e-books. I do not know whether this is true, but I do know a small number of authors have acquired contracts this way. Notice, I said a few, not thousands. So, some writers think by becoming indie authors they will be discovered. I wish them luck, but they will need the same amount of luck as they would need to win the National Lottery.

6. Independence and control.

I have left this reason until last because it is the reason I am an indie. As I have said previously, indie is short for independent, and I am a very independent person. The writers in this group want to control the whole process themselves. They want to be the ones making the decisions, deciding what to write and when to write it. But they must embrace the business side of the venture as well as the writing, not forgetting the hassle of marketing, distribution and promotion. However, the thing I love most about being an indie is the freedom it provides.

4

My Experience of the Indie World of Self-publishing

E-Publishing V Traditional Publishing

The world of publishing is undergoing changes as the electronic world catches up. As an author who has published both ways it seems to me to be a good time to weigh up the pros and cons.

My first book, the crime novel *Dead Wood*, was published in the traditional way after winning Britain's premier prize for debut novelists, the Dundee International Book Prize. What an exciting time that was. The procedure prior to publication was not without pain. Any author will tell you that writing 'The End' on the last page, is not really the end. There follows a period which can last up to a year or even longer, but in my case was eight months, for the editorial process. During this time conflicting demands were made – I had to add words and to cut words. The cover was decided by the publisher and the title was changed. But what a feeling of achievement there was when I held my book in my hands and saw it on the bookstore shelves with my name on the cover.

Now, all of the above may seem fairly easy to the new author, but that book had been hawked round publishers and agents for four years prior to winning the prize. Rejections were the order of the day. The last rejection I had was one month before winning the prize, and that publisher had retained the book for four years before making up his mind. That same publisher, I may add, had a recent column in a Sunday newspaper bemoaning the fact publishers were losing their authors to e-publishing.

So, two years later, after going through the same frustrating process of trying to interest publishers and agents in my second book, I decided to go down the electronic route and publish to Kindle. After the formatting it was relatively painless and cost me nothing, apart from the editing fee which is a good investment. Shortly after publishing to Kindle I published the book to Smashwords, an e-book distributor, so that readers could access my novel with other devices such as the Sony e-Reader, Kobo, Nook, and the Apple iPad. Admittedly, I did not have that wonderful feeling of holding a book in my hands, but at least it was out there and being read. After all, what is a writer without readers?

So what are the pros and cons? Well, with traditional publishing there is all the pain of constant rejections plus the length of time everything takes. With e-publishing the book can be on sale almost immediately, although I would advise sending it to a literary agency or editor prior to taking that step. A traditional publisher will pay 8 per cent royalties (average), while with e-publishing earnings can be anything between 35 to 85 per cent, provided you publish yourself. But best of all you are independent. The feeling of liberation is marvellous because you do not have to prostrate yourself to publishers.

I would say the e-publishing route has been a success for me, although I did miss being able to hold my book following publication. This was one of the reasons I decided to dip my toe into the paperback publishing waters, and now have paperbacks of my novels as well as e-books.

Adventures in CreateSpace
I have been publishing to Kindle since March 2011, with a

reasonable amount of success and with great satisfaction. Like many others before me I had come to the conclusion, that by pursuing a traditional deal with a traditional publisher, I was flogging, if not a dead horse, then certainly one not in the best of health. Therefore, I embarked wholeheartedly into the wonders of the electronic world of e-books.

So, now I am part of the electronic world, what on earth would induce me to return to the print world?

Well, my original decision stands – I am done with the traditional route to publish my books. However, I am often asked to talk to various readers' groups. I visit libraries, speak at conferences, do adjudications, and take an active role in professional writers' societies, such as the Society of Authors and the CWA (Crime Writers' Association). One thing that arose every time I gave a talk was, 'Where can we get the paperback?' And I always had to say, 'There is no paperback. Have you thought about getting an e-reader?' And that always came back with a resounding, 'No, we like paper books.'

Eventually I gave in. My readers were demanding paperbacks, so it was my job to provide them. Now, I knew that if I went back down the traditional route, the publisher would want my electronic rights as well. And that is something I never want to surrender. I am determined not to relinquish my electronic rights. So that only left one avenue – self-publishing.

In my experience there has always been a stigma around self-publishing, and I find authors who still publish the traditional way can be among the most disapproving. They forget many famous writers were originally self-published. Writers like – Mark Twain, Zane Grey, William Blake, Virginia Woolf, James Joyce, D H Lawrence, Edgar Rice Burroughs, George Bernard Shaw, Edgar Allan Poe, and Rudyard Kipling. Even Jane Austen self-published three of her novels – I could go on and on.

Maybe part of my reluctance to go down the paperback route was partly to do with that stigma because self-publishing on Kindle did not really seem like self-publishing in the true sense of the word, but if I published a paperback I would truly be a self-publisher.

My desire to satisfy my readers soon overcame that last vestige of reluctance, and I looked about to see how I could do it. The one proviso I gave myself was that I would not pay for my book to be published because to me that smacked of vanity publishing, something with an even greater stigma. So I looked around the POD (print on demand) publishers and settled on Amazon's CreateSpace, although I had heard that having books shipped from the US is very expensive.

I found the procedure relatively simple by using one of the templates CreateSpace make available. I copied and pasted my book into the template, chapter by chapter, as per instructions, but the biggest decision at this point was the font. Which one would I use? I tried several but the ones I liked did not have curly quotes, and I do like them curly! So I came back to the tried and tested Times New Roman with a two point leading which formats extra space between the lines. This enhances the reading experience because the text is not crammed together.

I did not take CreateSpace's advice on the most popular format, because when I looked round my bookshelves I could not find any books that were size 6 x 9 with white pages. Books were mostly 8 x 5 inches or 8.5 x 5.5 inches, and they all had cream pages. I decided on the 8.5 x 5.5 size with cream pages, and the resulting book exceeded my expectations.

The next stage was to decide whether I wanted a CreateSpace ISBN which is supplied free, but it makes CreateSpace the publisher. Now, being the independent person I am, otherwise known as an awkward sod, I decided I did not want to be beholden to CreateSpace, so I went the alternative route and bought my own ISBNs.

I particularly liked the CreateSpace digital proofer, an online tool, which allows you to see how the actual book will look when it is published. I also found the downloadable PDF useful; this sets the manuscript out like a book. It made the inspection and proofing relatively easy. However, I did order a physical proof before approving the book.

Once my first book was on stream as a paperback I went ahead and did the same for the others. So now I have four paperback novels available as well as my Kindle versions, and the strange thing is, there has been an increase of Kindle sales since the paperbacks became available.

There was one other surprise. When I ordered my first twenty author copies from CreateSpace they came in cheaper than the author copies I get from my mainstream publisher. And that was despite the cost of postage from the US. However, I do not understand why the CreateSpace author copies have to be despatched from the US when customers buying them in this country are provided with UK copies. The mysteries of Amazon!

So, what are my expectations from sales of the paperback? I have no great expectations; I do not think they will sell in shed-loads. I only brought them on as a service to my readers. My heart is still with electronic publishing.

5

Introduction to Crime Fiction Subgenres

Crime in all its aspects has always intrigued me, and I think I have been reading crime fiction and non-fiction most of my adult life. I even went to the extent of studying for a qualification in criminology.

So what is it about crime that fascinates me so much? Well, to put it simply, it is my way of trying to understand what makes the criminal what he or she is, but sooner or later it comes back to the nature/nurture argument. Are criminals born to commit crime; or is it the influence of their parents, the type of parenting they had, the influences of their peer group, or what? I honestly don't think there is an easy answer, but the mindset of people who commit crimes is something I endeavour to understand.

Of course, there have been various theories over the years. There were the physiological and biological theories which indicated a criminal could be identified by his appearance. Llombroso, the Italian criminologist (1835-1909), believed criminals were evolutionary throwbacks whose physical features included enormous jaws, high cheekbones, and apelike features. At one time it was believed that feeling the bumps on a human head could reveal whether or not that person was a criminal. If only it were so easy! The biological theories in respect of criminology have now been largely discredited, but elements linger on in eugenics as well as some popular ideas that ethnicity is linked to criminality. This is illustrated in the belief of some ethnic groups that they suffer from discrimination as well as police harassment, for example, the police stop and search practice which it is claimed targets more black people than white.

I find psychological theories of most interest. There are humanistic, behavioural, and cognitive theories, through which crime and the criminal can be studied. And we are back to nature and nurture with a bit of conditioning thrown in for good measure. But I am sure you do not want to know all the different theories, and which of those theories should take precedence when we consider criminals and crime. It is enough to state the study of the criminal and the crimes they commit continue to interest many people. Maybe that is the reason we read crime fiction and non-fiction. On the other hand, maybe it is because we like a puzzle to solve.

I gave much thought to what would be of interest in a study of crime writing in all its aspects, and came to the conclusion I would study a spectrum of crime fiction. But where would I start?

One of the main elements of most crime novels is mystery. The story has to keep the reader guessing. So what better place to begin. Then I plan to work my way through the genres starting with mystery and cosy crime (or cozy crime, as our American friends spell it). So, my first topic will be mystery.

But I did not want to discuss the authors everyone has heard about. I wanted new authors, the independent ones known as indies, and I wanted to explore what was on offer. I realize I cannot cover every author who has ever published an e-book so that meant I would have to compile a reading list, and I wanted the selection to be fairly random, maybe some authors I had vaguely heard about, plus a decent smattering of ones I knew nothing about.

There are many online stores selling e-books, but Amazon is one of the largest so that was where I started. This is by no means a recommendation of Amazon, nor am I advocating you buy your e-books from this company, but there are more people reading on Amazon's Kindle than any other type of e-reader, so it made sense to use their database of e-books. This was why I set about my task by checking the Amazon lists for different kinds of crime fiction. After compiling a list of possible titles I visited independent review sites and blogs to garner recommendations. This is relatively easy to do by searching, or googling, the title of the book followed by the word review. Following this I returned to Amazon to read their reviews, and I used the 'Look Inside' feature to make a snap judgement about the quality of the e-book. Then I built my list of authors and books. Now this can be risky because, although there are many excellent books published electronically, there can be some books that are less well written. So, I decided if I hit any of the latter I would read no further than was necessary in order to make a decision, and would not include them in this study.

I would like to point out that the books I include are my choices, which may or may not appeal to everyone, but I hope it will encourage readers to explore of the world of indie fiction, and I am sure they will not be disappointed.

However genres overlap, so where I might be introducing you to a mystery novel, it is possible it could also be categorized as a supernatural crime, or a police procedural.

But firstly, what is the definition of crime fiction? It is necessary to understand this before attempting to define the subgenres.

6
What is Crime Fiction?

Defining crime fiction was not such an easy task as I had assumed. I thought I knew what a crime novel was. It had to be a novel that featured crime, any kind of crime, from petty theft through to murder, pulling in fraud and corporate crime along the way. That seemed logical to me. But that was before I started trawling the internet for definitions of crime fiction, and succeeded in confusing myself, and questioning whether I was actually a crime writer.

The reason for my confusion arose from the many definitions of what I thought was crime, appearing under the heading of thrillers. A lot of the material referred to crime fiction as mystery, and the definitions were related to what I would term the traditional mystery, the type of story Arthur Conan Doyle or Agatha Christie might have written. This gives the impression crime fiction has not moved on and has become stuck in the early twentieth century.

A comparatively new and expensive addition to my reference library, *The Readers' Advisory Guide to Genre Fiction*, by Joyce G. Saricks, does not even have a section on crime fiction. The nearest categories she uses are Mysteries, Suspense, and Thrillers.

The definition Saricks offers for the mystery novel is: *"Mysteries consist of a puzzle: the author provides the clues to the solution but attempts to obscure some information so that the puzzle cannot be solved too easily. We, along with the detective, are drawn into the puzzle in an attempt to solve it.*

This puzzle involves a crime, usually murder, and the resulting body. There is an investigator (or a team of investigators) amateur or professional, who solves the question of 'who-dun-it.' The Mystery tracks this investigation, with its concomitant exploration of victim's, murderer's, and detective's lives."

So, what does Saricks say about thrillers: *"Basically this genre focuses on a particular profession - espionage, medical, or legal, for example - and tells an action packed story that reveals the intricacies of that profession and the potential dangers faced by those involved in it."* However, she goes on to say there are shared elements with suspense, adventure, and mystery genres, and that it is *"a gripping, plot-centered story."* Well, at least that last bit is something it shares with crime fiction.

My trawl of the internet did not reveal much in the way of definitions for crime fiction. If I wanted to look at this genre, a search for mystery was more successful. Thrillers brought many more results, although a lot of the definitions were equally applicable to crime fiction. It made me wonder whether crime fiction as a genre was being swallowed up by the thriller genre. Or maybe this is a British, American thing, with the Brits referring to the genre as crime fiction and the Americans using the thriller genre. Certainly, many writers referred to as thriller writers I would have termed crime writers. Authors such as, Ed McBain, Robert Crais, Michael Connolly, Patricia Cornwell, Kathy Reichs, and many more. I even found Agatha Christie, and Arthur Conan Doyle, the creator of Sherlock Holmes, listed as thriller writers.

The Online Free Dictionary, defines thriller as *"a book, film, play etc., depicting crime, mystery, or espionage in an atmosphere of excitement and suspense."* I could not find a definition for crime fiction in the dictionary, but it defines murder mystery as *"a narrative about a murder and how the murderer is discovered."*

James Patterson, in the introduction to *Thriller: Stories to keep you up all night,* writes that thrillers cover a wide spectrum which he calls a literary feast, *"The legal thriller, spy thriller, action-adventure thriller, medical thriller, police thriller, historical thriller, political thriller, religious thriller, high-tech thriller, military thriller. The list goes on and on, with new variations constantly being invented."* The thriller, therefore, seems to cover a great deal of ground. But hang on a minute. In the middle of that list is the police thriller. Now surely that must be crime fiction! Patterson goes on to say *"By definition, if a thriller doesn't thrill, it's not doing its job."* Well, at least I am in agreement with him there.

By this time you will realize why I was starting to question what kind of writer I am. I have always classed myself as a crime writer, and I certainly fit the criteria of having a puzzle to solve in my books. However, I am also an action writer and I like to use suspense to build tension, and that fits more comfortably into the thriller category. So, am I a crime writer or a thriller writer, or a mix of both?

I am not the only one suffering from confusion. There is an excellent article in Hunter Emkay's blog, *Hunting Down Writing,* which is titled *Mysteries Vs Thrillers Vs Crime Fiction,* well worth reading, if only to get a taste of the confusion that abounds between the genres.

In my search for crime fiction definitions the only ones I found were buried in the middle of articles, mainly written by British writers.

Here is a quote from *The Strange Appeal of Crime Fiction,* written by Andrew Taylor, a well known British author, *"Most - though not all - crime novels share a common structure. First there is the crime, usually a murder; then there is the investigation; and finally the resolution or judgement, often in the shape of the criminal's arrest or death. This tight structure is another reason for the genre's appeal. "*

Another quote I found, written by author, Rachel Marsh, reads *"Crime stories are about someone committing an immoral or illegal act (plenty of Agatha Christie's short stories were about theft, not murder), and someone else attempting to bring them to justice. I think it is the second aspect, 'someone else attempting to bring them to justice' that is essential, because plenty of literature has characters committing immoral acts, yet they are not classified as crime fiction. "*

The Ask Jeeves web site came up with the following definition, *"Crime fiction is an enormously and modern genre of fiction that deals with crime, crime recognition, criminals and their causes. Its common structure is usually crime first then investigation and lastly judgement either in arrest or death. There are also other genres of fiction used in artistic literature like science fiction or historical fiction. "*

Now that I have explored the internet as well as several guides to genre fiction, I think it is time to consult the reference book I find most valuable. This reference book on crime fiction was originally published in 1999, and it is my constant companion. It is *The Oxford Companion to Crime & Mystery Writing,* edited by Rosemary Herbert. It covers every aspect of crime fiction you can imagine, features many crime writers, and provides the historical basis of crime fiction.

First of all I want to look at what it says about thrillers. Surprisingly, it states something which is the exact opposite of everything I have been reading about thrillers. The thriller is actually a subtype of crime and mystery writing with its roots in the world of pulp fiction. They were known as dime novels in the United States, and as bloods, shockers, and penny dreadfuls in Britain. In the introduction to the thriller section it states: *"'Thriller' entered British usage in the final quarter of the nineteenth century in reference to stories of heroic adventure set in criminal situations. In their plots of contest, thrillers bore a relationship to heroic romance, their rendition of sinister villains and atmosphere indicated their kinship to the Gothic novel, and their use of criminal matter and lowlife detail classed them with the popular police memoirs of the time."* *(John M. Reilly and Clive Bloom).* Moving on from thrillers I wonder how my reference book will define crime fiction.

There was a large entry on the crime novel, and much more about the history of crime fiction which I will deal with later. The crime novel entry stated: *"The term 'crime novel' has come into general use increasingly in the last two decades, but it is inevitably imprecise since the label can be applied to any tale involving detection or criminal violence. Yet in practice the term marks out important areas of differentiation, particularly between a story concerned primarily with discovering the identity of a criminal and one dealing chiefly with criminal psychology and the reasons for the crime. The difference is between the whodunit and the whydunit. At the heart of the detective story is a puzzle, while the core of the crime novel is a criminal's character."* *(Julian Symons).*

I have found the exploration through crime fiction and thrillers to be fascinating. On the one hand thriller definitions include all the subgenres I am applying to crime fiction, and yet reading British sources these subgenres belong firmly within crime fiction. This reassures me because I write psychological crime fiction with a police procedural element, and they are action based page turners. This was leading me to believe I might be a thriller writer rather than the crime writer I have always considered myself to be. On the other hand, if the thriller and crime fiction genres have merged, perhaps the description of my books might be termed crime thrillers. I will have to think about that.

7

A Short History of Crime Fiction

Development

It is difficult to assess how far back the origins of crime fiction go, and it is possible we will never know. Some historians, for example, view *Oedipus Rex*, a story about incest, murder and suicide which was written by Sophocles and first performed around 429 BC as one of the first stories about crime.

I intend to concentrate on a period stretching from the eighteenth and nineteenth centuries beginning with *The Newgate Calendar*, subtitled *The Malefactors' Bloody Register*, which was a popular work during this period. This publication started out as a monthly bulletin of executions produced by the Keeper of Newgate Prison. However, it was soon followed by the production of chapbooks about notorious criminals such as Dick Turpin, and Sawney Bean. Then there were books about thief catchers. After the Bow Street Runners were established in 1748, stories about the Runners became popular. Similarly, when a uniformed police force came into being in 1829, Charles Dickens based a series of articles, published between 1850 to 1870, on the detective police.

It seemed the reading public could not get enough of sensationalism, and a variety of writers produced fictional memoirs, including Allan Pinkerton of the Pinkerton Detective Agency in the US. This was also the time of the dime novels which started to appear in the 1870s. The crime based ones featured amateur and private detectives as well as police characters. One of the writers associated with dime novels was

Nick Carter, although this was a pseudonym for many writers hiding behind the Carter name. The equivalent in Britain was the Sexton Blake series which commenced in 1893, and was written for boys' magazines. It is thought Sexton Blake lived through more than four thousand adventures, written by over two hundred writers. These examples are the historical equivalent of today's book packagers who use multiple authors to write series books.

Detective fiction made its debut during this period as the writing changed, from a style that was meant to create shock and horror, to tighter plots and more literary stories. The change must have been gradual, although it is thought the works of Edgar Allan Poe introduced the new writing style. *The Murders in the Rue Morgue*, published in 1841, is often quoted as the first mystery novel. This was closely followed by *The Mystery of Marie Roget*, in 1842, and *The Purloined Letter*, in 1845. Many writers embraced detective fiction in the latter part of the nineteenth century, and among the better known were Joseph Sheridan le Fanu, and Wilkie Collins.

The rising popularity of crime and mystery fiction in the late nineteenth century is said to be illustrated by the popularity of *The Mystery of a Hansom Cab*, written by Fergus Hume in 1886. I had never heard of this book which was apparently a blockbuster, and it set me wondering how a late nineteenth century bestseller would compare with today's crime novels.

Landmarks in the development of detective fiction during the latter part of the nineteenth century and the early years of the twentieth, were Edgar Allan Poe's *The Murders in the Rue Morgue* (previously mentioned), and Arthur Conan Doyle's *A Study in Scarlet*, in 1887. Following the publication of his first novel, Conan Doyle published 56 Sherlock Holmes stories, and four novellas between 1887 and 1892, and is attributed with introducing a series character and his sidekick – Holmes and

Watson. Detective fiction continued to expand during this period with other writers following the lead Conan Doyle had set. It is an era of the great detective solving mysteries with the aid of an assistant.

However, as the detective story rose in popularity other novels were published using a similar formula, but featuring the adventures of master criminals. It was during this time the first stories appeared, featuring E. W. Hornung's creation, Raffles, the gentleman thief. Gentlemen thieves seemed to be a popular concept, with Maurice Leblanc introducing his character, Arsene Lupin, in 1907. Another popular series was based on the adventures of the master criminal Fu Manchu, written by Sax Rohmer.

Moving on to the period between the two world wars in the twentieth century, detective fiction continued to flourish, and this has been labelled the golden age of crime and mystery writing.

This golden age of crime fiction emphasized the puzzle element of detective stories. They were considered intellectual exercises, and writers of these stories distanced themselves from the type of sensational action stories to be found in pulp magazines. The focus was on the puzzle, while descriptions and characterization were thought to be unnecessary. This may explain why the main criticism of Agatha Christie's crime novels, focuses on the two dimensional nature of her characters.

Golden age authors

Many of the golden age authors continued to use series characters, and in the case of Agatha Christie she had several series characters in the books she produced.

1920 saw the introduction of Hercule Poirot by Agatha Christie in *The Mysterious Affair at Styles*. She followed this with Tuppence and Tommy Beresford in *The Secret Adversary* in 1922, and then with Jane Marple in 1930, in *The Murder at the Vicarage*.

1923 – Dorothy L. Sayers, introduced Lord Peter Wimsey in *Whose Body*.

1929 – Margery Allingham published *The Crime at Black Dudley*, featuring Albert Campion.

1929 – Josephine Tey, writing under the pseudonym Gordon Daviot, published *The Man in the Queue*, featuring her series character Inspector Alan Grant.

1934 – Ngaio Marsh introduced Superintendent Roderick Alleyn, in *A Man Lay Dead*.

Well known male golden age authors in Britain include: Nicholas Blake; Michael Innes; Philip MacDonald; and the American born John Dickson Carr, who was considered the master of the locked room mystery.

The golden age authors in the United States included: Willard Huntington Wright, whose pseudonym was S. S. Van Dine; Frederic Dannay writing as Ellery Queen; and Manfred B. Lee writing under the name of Barnaby Ross, as well as many others.

The golden age also saw the birth of the tough, gritty genre of hard-boiled crime fiction in the United States; stories featuring tough detectives with a bottle of whisky in the filing cabinet and a glamorous dame seeking their help. This may have been linked with prohibition and the gangster ethos this brought about.

Hard-boiled crime fiction, and private eyes, appeared initially in the pulp and dime magazines, and the names most easily recognized are Dashiell Hammett, and Raymond Chandler. However, hard-boiled writing was in direct opposition to the classical golden age style of detective fiction as it was tougher and more realistic, with better characterization.

Another style of writing, which developed between the two

world wars, introduced characters who operated outside the law. John Creasey created The Toff, an amateur sleuth and detective who appeared in fifty-nine novels. Creasey was a prolific writer who wrote more than six hundred novels, under twenty-eight different pseudonyms. It would be unrealistic to include all his characters, but I am sure readers will remember The Baron, and Gideon of Scotland Yard.

Other writers using similar characters include: Bruce Graeme, with Blackshirt; and Leslie Charteris, with The Saint. It could even be said Ian Fleming's James Bond fits this profile, although the Bond books were written later on, in the 1950s.

By the end of the second world war the hard-boiled detective stories, which originated in the United States, were gaining popularity. It was the age of the private eye and a move into the darker world of crime. Mickey Spillane created his detective, Mike Hammer, in *I The Jury*, in 1947, and Ross Macdonald introduced Lew Archer in 1949, in *The Moving Target*. However, Hammett and Chandler had been writing hard-boiled, private eye fiction twenty years earlier so they would have to be considered the forerunners of this genre.

The police procedural first appeared in the United States in 1945, with Lawrence Treat's *V as in Victim*. Six years later in 1951, British writer, Maurice Proctor published *The Chief Inspector's Statement*, also known as *The Pennycross Murders*. These books altered the form of the traditional detective story by replacing the detective with a team of police officers, and bringing in the procedural nature of investigations. The police procedural format was adopted by writers such as Hilary Waugh and Ed McBain in America, and in Britain by John Creasey who published his *Gideon of Scotland Yard* series under the pen name of J.J. Marric. The first of these books *Gideon's Day*, was published in 1955. The police procedural remains popular to the present day.

A further diversification in the form of the mystery novel was the increasing importance of characterization, and the appearance of novels with no detectives or clues. Psychology, characterization and motive, are the driving forces of these novels, and examples can be found in the works of authors such as Patricia Highsmith and Barbara Vine.

So where is the crime or mystery novel today? It is safe to say the genre continues to develop. Hard-boiled detectives are still macho, although no longer restricted to white American tough guys, and they may now display a softer side. Ethnic groups are no longer excluded as detectives, and there are women detectives, as well as gay and lesbian sleuths.

The traditional mystery story is still being written, but has become known as the cosy. Some of the newer subgenres to appear include: historical detective stories; legal procedurals or thrillers; political thrillers; forensic thrillers; and many other variations of the crime and mystery genre. It is these subgenres I will be discussing in the following chapters.

8

Mystery in Crime Fiction

Mystery is not exclusive to crime fiction. It can be found in many other genres, and the mystery in these books may not necessarily be linked to crime. However, mystery is one of the most important elements of many crime stories where it is necessary to keep the reader guessing.

The importance of this factor in crime fiction was enhanced during the golden age of the classic detective novel, and the genre became known as the mystery and detective genre during this time. The title has stuck, and many crime books are still known as mystery and detective, although the crime genre has developed substantially over the years.

If we consider mystery in these terms it would seem to relate more to the type of novel based on deduction – the style of story that Agatha Christie was so good at writing. There have been many other novels which fit into the mystery category, not least, Wilkie Collins with *The Woman in White* which features crime and mystery in a story of fortune hunting and changed identities.

However, it is difficult to think about crime fiction without considering the part mystery plays in a good novel, for this is the main component in this type of fiction. But there are exceptions, mainly in some of the newer and more modern forms of crime stories. For the moment, I will concentrate on the role of mystery.

While studying crime fiction as a genre I noticed that any time mystery was mentioned it was invariably linked with detection, as a mystery and detective genre. This indicates that mystery, as part of the genre, stands for the puzzle element in a crime novel, and the solving of that puzzle by detection. It requires the participation of the reader in the deductive process, and it is a component of the classic detective novel of the golden age which concentrated on the intellectual aspects of solving crimes rather than the sensational stories of earlier times.

H.R.F. Keating, when describing the classical design of a crime story, in his book *Writing Crime Fiction*, says *"The blueprint of a detective story at its most basic is not a story. It is a static puzzle. Someone has been murdered in mysterious circumstances: how has it come about. But this basic situation, in order to be made into something which people will have pleasure in reading, has to be seen in exactly the opposite light, as the gradual making clear of things. In other words, as a story."*

I like to think that the meaning of mystery is wider than that, and you can have mystery in most crime fiction, not just in the whodunit. No doubt there is a great deal of mystery involved when the identity of the killer is unknown, and the puzzle has to be solved. But I also believe that mystery is involved in the whydunit where the focus is on why the murder was committed and the psychology of the murderer and other characters in the story.

Life is full of mystery, so it follows that mystery in crime fiction is spread wider than the mystery and detective genre. As a result this leaves us with a wide range of crime novels, including the cosy as well as the darker varieties of crime, that rub covers on our bookshelves, virtual or otherwise. However, if we take the narrower view of mystery in crime fiction, the nearest subgenre is probably the cosy because it is modelled on the classic detective stories that preceded the birth of a variety of other categories of crime stories.

Mystery and crime fiction is one of the most popular genres with readers. Barbara Norville, editor, publisher, and teacher, has stated that half the books on the *New York Times* Best Sellers list are murder mysteries.

The mystery story, it seems, has never lost favour with readers since it was introduced to the reading public by Edgar Allan Poe's, *Murders in the Rue Morgue*. There was nothing cosy about that tale! The baton was then taken up by Arthur Conan Doyle, with his *Sherlock Holmes* stories, and it has been continued by a variety of crime writers ever since.

Taking into consideration the wide ranging nature of mystery in fiction presented a problem to me when I considered my reading list. What should I choose to illustrate mystery writing that would do justice to the genre? I could have taken an example from police procedurals, particularly the whodunits, or I could have chosen historical, medical, legal, or psychological (whydunits), or any of the other categories. However, for my first choices I settled on two books by the same author which have a definite sense of mystery, but which could also be categorized as cosy, or similar to the classic detective story.

The e-books I chose were Myra Duffy's two mystery novels set in Bute, an island off the west coast of Scotland. I chose them because they contained a distinct sense of mystery right from the start. There is no gore in these books, no bloodstained corpses, although there are bodies. But they were a nice, non-taxing gentle read. Although 'gentle read' and 'crime novel' seem to be contradictory terms.

The first of these books was *The House at Ettrick Bay*. What I liked about this book was the steady build up of mystery. It had all the ingredients – a mysterious, gloomy house, an archaeological dig, a vague feeling of threat, and an amateur detective, all combined with secrets and the sins of the past.

The second book *Last Ferry to Bute*, was a follow up with the same amateur detective, the same sense of mystery, although it did not build up quite so quickly as the previous book. The setting was Bute again, and I know Bute, so it was a nice feeling revisiting the island in a novel. No gloomy mysterious houses this time, but a suspicious care home, antiques and, of course, some bodies. This second book was well edited but did have some minor formatting glitches (a few irregular paragraph indents probably due to the conversion process), not enough to intrude into the reading experience, and my interest in the story made them irrelevant. I have to say at this point I have read several books published by mainstream publishing houses where the formatting was much worse.

Both of these books were well written with good plots, and the characters came alive on the page. This is an author who knows how to tell a good story.

In my search for a third book I came across *The Filey Connection*, which is the first book in the Sanford Third Age Club Mystery series, by David W Robinson.

This is a mystery story, which would probably be considered a cosy. It was quite a pleasant read, but I felt there was too much emphasis on the characters at the beginning of the book, and it was quite a long time before the action started. However, the characters were well drawn and believable as members of a third age club.

Joe, the main character, reminded me of a male Miss Marple. He pokes about, finding out what he can, and then shares it with a police chief inspector who defers to him and values his contribution. I found his relationship with the police somewhat unrealistic, although it was much the same investigative methods Agatha Christie's Miss Marple used. These methods may have been acceptable at the time Agatha Christie was writing her books, they are less believable in a contemporary crime novel. But readers will probably like this book if their taste is for a nice gentle murder mystery read, reminiscent of an earlier age.

I bought *The Assassins' Village* by Faith Mortimer, because of the crime element, and it was described as a classic detective story, so I was expecting something similar to an Agatha Christie book that would fit neatly into my mystery section. But it was far more than that. It was a character study and a literary feast. The descriptive passages were so real I could imagine I was walking down a dusty road in the heat of a Cyprus summer, and I shared the lives of the characters.

There are a lot of characters in this book and when I started reading I found this a bit confusing. However, it wasn't long before I got so engrossed in all the characters' lives that I couldn't wait to find out more about them. I found the cultural differences between the expats and the Cypriot natives, fascinating. It was like living in the modern age and in a historical time warp all at the same time.

The build up to the murder was gradual, and it became obvious who the victim would be, but not so obvious who was going to do it. And this was where the book differed from a classical detective story, where the murder takes place, and the sleuth does the detecting. This murder was committed nearer to the middle of the book rather than the beginning, although there was a prologue to alert you that something murderous was going to happen.

The mystery in this book was built up through the character studies and the sense that a murder was imminent.

My enjoyment in this book was two-fold. I enjoyed the murder-mystery element, but I also enjoyed the character driven storyline. This is a novel that bookstores would need little convincing to include on their shelves.

On the whole, these books were all well written, and a print version would not have been out of place in a bookshop. They fulfilled the criteria of mystery in crime fiction and, apart from *The Assassins' Village*, they were similar in structure to the classic or traditional detective mystery novel. Are they better than traditionally published novels? Well, I suppose that is a matter of taste, I certainly thought they were a match for many books currently published in the traditional way.

In my next chapter I will be looking at the cosy crime novel, which is similar in many ways to the traditional mystery novel.

9
the Cosy Mystery

The word cosy conjures up images of comfort, warmth and security. Crime, on the other hand, indicates something much darker, and in the world of crime fiction it suggests violence, murder, alienation, and all sorts of actions which are the opposite of cosy. So cosy is a strange adjective to use to describe a crime genre and is a contradiction in terms when considering crime fiction.

Cosy and mystery are words which became linked in the latter half of the twentieth century by writers seeking to emulate the golden age of detective fiction. Books written by these authors became known as cosy mysteries, and the new subgenre which was created is closely related to the novels of these earlier writers. So, if you associate cosy with something relaxing and pleasant, as the word suggests, then think again. There are murders, violence and crime in cosy mysteries, although much of the violence takes place off the page and is not explicit.

One thing the cosy has in common with most crime fiction is mystery. It must have something that requires to be investigated, usually by an amateur rather than a professional. If you think about Miss Marple, you have a perfect example of the type of investigator these mysteries have. However, there are the exceptions, like Hamish Macbeth, where a policeman is the sleuth, but these policemen are more like the traditional village bobby, than the up to date professional and forensically aware police officer of more recent crime novels. So, there is something inherently old-fashioned about cosies.

In the *Oxford Companion to Crime & Mystery Writing*, the section on Cozy Mystery (interestingly this British reference book uses the American spelling) says, *"A term first used in the Observer 25 May 1958, 'cozy' refers to a subgenre of the novel of detection defined by its light tone, element of fun, and closed world."* It goes on to describe what kind of mystery this is. It needs a detective who may be either an amateur or a professional. The suspects are usually known to each other, and the plot is intricate.

Cosy mysteries are usually gentler than many other crime novels, such as the police procedural. There is no graphic violence, swearing, or explicit sex. If there is sex, it takes place behind closed doors.

The cosy mystery is all about puzzle solving. In most cases, it is a whodunit with clues and red herrings to assist the reader in finding out the identity of the murderer before the writer reveals all. In many ways it is similar to the classic detective novels of an earlier time.

As for the setting, it is usually a small community, often with a rural or village setting, and never concentrates on the dark underbelly of city crime. There are rarely gangsters, drug users, or prostitutes. Likewise, the murderers are never psychopaths or serial killers, and when arrested, they go quietly. They are usually members of the community where the crime is committed, and the motives are those of greed, revenge, or jealousy.

The murders are generally bloodless, and the gritty details of the body are rarely described apart from giving the cause of death. Agatha Christie was particularly fond of poisoning.

Contemporary authors who write books which would fall into the category of cosy crime include, Alexander McCall Smith, Simon Brett, M. C. Beaton, and J. K. Rowling writing as

Robert Galbraith.

In my quest for e-books which could be described as cosy, I managed to find a few. The first one I downloaded was *Crime in the Community,* by Cecilia Peartree. I had never read anything by her before, and all I knew about this author was that she came from the Edinburgh area. So the Scottish connection influenced my choice.

Crime in the Community was a good read. I loved the characters, members of a community group in the village of Pitkirtly. Their interaction with each other and those they came into contact with was fascinating as they fought progress and tried to keep their group as a small talking shop with its main focus on the alcohol they could consume. However, a new village member, a retired spy of all things, infiltrates their group and suddenly everything changes. Christopher, the chairman of the group, is involved in mysterious goings-on and the group are pulled into the thick of it. One element missing from this story was a body, although there was an 'almost murder' which did not get carried through. So, although it met all the criteria for a cosy mystery novel – the small community, amateur sleuth, criminal activity etc, I am not entirely sure it qualified as a cosy crime. I do not think there is such a thing as a cosy thriller, but that is what I would be tempted to call it.

My next choice was *The Woolly Murders,* by Milly Reynolds. I am ambivalent about this book. It was well written, and the plot was good, but somehow or other it did not grab me to the same extent as my previous choice. Maybe it was because the first murder victims were sheep. Their fleeces were being stolen and they were being hurt, and then as the killer got a taste for it, he was killing them for no apparent reason. He did progress to killing people, but by that time I think the sheep had got to me. I did wonder if it was a send up of serial killing, but I wasn't sure. The main character of this one was a policeman who had transferred from a larger police force to a small town, and he did seem to assume the role of village bobby quite nicely, but as an avid reader of police procedurals I doubt if his method of working would fit into the modern police force. However, it did tick the boxes of a cosy, and it had a good plot. If you like your crime to be the cosy type, and do not mind the killing of animals, you might find this more interesting than I did.

My third book was *The Temporary Detective,* by Joanne Sydney Lessner, and once I started to read I was surprised to discover this was an American book. I have read many American authors, and I like their style, which is quite different from most British writing. But I had not previously linked American authors to cosy crime. However, after further investigation, I discovered this is a popular genre in the US.

I loved this book. I thought it an enjoyable light read, probably ideal for the beach, or to read on a journey. It had all the elements of a cosy – an amateur detective, a mystery to solve, a whodunit, no graphic sex or violence, although it was hinted at in the book, and being a more modern cosy it did not shy away from characters who were gay, or cross dressers. The setting was New York, which it could be argued, was not a small community. However, the action took place in the offices of a company which did meet the criteria of a closed community. Above all, it had humour, as well as likeable and realistic characters. This was the first book of a series, so I will be watching out for the publication of the next one.

The last book I read for this section was *Murderer's Fete* by Roger Keevil. This was a classic detective mystery with touches of humour. I liked the play on names. There was an Inspector Constable, and a Sergeant Copper. The lady of the house, who was also a Justice of the Peace, was Lady Lawdown. The solicitor was Robin Allday. There was also an author whose pen name was Jake A Rawlings, and she wrote books about a schoolgirl magician, Carrie Otter. The titles of her books were Carrie Otter and the Photographers Stain, Carie Otter and the Half Boiled Pants, and Carrie Otter and the Deadly Pillows. This play on names added a light touch and made the book resemble a parody, although the plot followed the lines of the classic or traditional murder mystery.

The setting was one that is in frequent use in Midsomer Murders type mysteries. There was the village of Dammett Worthy, the parish church, and Dammett Hall, the home of Lady Lawdown, where the action takes place. Everyone in this book had secrets, and while it was comparatively easy to guess some of the secrets, the plot was sufficiently convoluted to keep me guessing.

The book was well written, edited, and formatted. It started life as a dinner theatre murder mystery which didn't surprise me. I found it an easy, non-taxing read with good, natural dialogue, which would be ideal for reading on a journey or relaxing on a beach.

My reading for this topic was satisfying, and the books I chose were a good fit for the cosy mystery definition. They were well written and plotted, and they compared well with traditionally published books in the same genre.

I will be looking at something different in the next section. A type of mystery novel that I had not previously included as a crime novel, and a category that does not seem to be universally recognized, in Britain, as belonging to crime fiction – romantic suspense.

10

Romantic Suspense

Romantic suspense is a crime category I had not been aware of until I heard an author talking about it on a panel at Crimefest. This convention which is held annually at Bristol, focuses on crime books and writers, so this made me think that perhaps this type of crime fiction might be worthy of further exploration. My initial investigation into the genre confirmed that romantic suspense is not widely recognized in the UK as crime fiction, although it is a popular genre in the US. However, I did mention the genre to a friend who writes contemporary romance novels, and she not only knew what romantic suspense is, but she gave me the impression that this is a well known category of romance. So, that begs the question, as to whether romantic suspense is a subgenre of romance or of crime. And whether crime writers back away from romance in their thrillers, although I have read many crime books with a thread of romantic interest in them.

I set out to look for definitions of romantic suspense, and consulted the two volumes which are my bibles on crime fiction. But there was no mention of romantic suspense in *The Oxford Companion to Crime & Mystery Writing*, edited by Rosemary Herbert, nor was there anything in *British Crime Writing: An Encyclopedia*, by Barry Forshaw. It was time to turn to Google.

I did identify some definitions on the internet, but I also found reference to a book titled, *The Readers' Advisory Guide to Genre Fiction*, written by Joyce G Saricks, as a guide to help librarians make recommendations to readers. This book was quite expensive, and I had to think seriously about whether I would buy it or not. But I am a hopelessly addicted bookaholic, so I bought it, justifying my purchase as being in the interests of research. This book made a great addition to my ever increasing library of reference books, and it had sections on many of the genres that are familiar to readers. For the time being, however, I was interested in the section on romantic suspense.

Saricks introduces this section with the sentence – *"Before the line 'It was a dark and stormy night' became a cliché, it was the phrase that epitomized the Gothic novel, the forerunner of the Romantic Suspense genre."* That gave me pause to think. I would never have associated the gothic novel with romantic suspense. In my mind it was associated with horror, depicted in novels like *Dracula, Frankenstein, The Fall of the House of Usher*, and *The Castle of Otranto*. These novels seemed a far cry from romantic suspense. However, in looking further at some of these novels, there is a distinct romantic thread running through them all, and Mary Shelley, the author of *Frankenstein*, was part of the romantic movement in the nineteenth century. Some classic nineteenth century romance novels, such as *Wuthering Heights*, by Emily Bronte, and Charlotte Bronte's *Jane Eyre*, could also be described as gothic novels, as well as Daphne du Maurier's novel *Rebecca*, written in the twentieth century. So, maybe the link between gothic and romantic suspense is not so strange after all, although before we leave gothic fiction it might be as well to look at a couple of definitions.

Definitions of Gothic Romance:

Free Online Dictionary – *"a romance that deals with desolate and mysterious and grotesque events."*

Britannica Concise Encyclopedia – *"gothic novel. European Romantic, pseudo-medieval fiction with a prevailing* atmosphere of mystery and terror. Such novels were often set in castles or monasteries equipped with subterranean passages, dark battlements, and hidden panels, and they had plots involving ghosts, madness, outrage, superstition, and revenge."

Romantic suspense, stating the obvious, is a combination of romance and suspense using elements of crime, mystery, danger, adventure, and even espionage. It must have female and male main characters, and a villain, and is often told from the female point of view. They are fast paced with a build up of suspense, and often depict graphic sexual scenes. Saricks says – "Although Traditional Romantic Suspense is softer edged, generally leaving bodies offstage, Contemporary Romantic Suspense may present graphic details, as well as strong language and explicit sexual descriptions."

I had enjoyed reading Saricks' section on romantic suspense, but I wanted to explore other definitions, so I went on a search for what other people had to say, and I will list several examples I found, although they all seemed to be rather similar.

Laura Sheehan, an author, writes that 'danger' is the defining element of romantic suspense. However, she goes on to say there is "a central love story in which the lovers have to traverse a perilous plot of nail-biting adventures."

Author, Deirdre Savoy says – "Many people believe that any romance that includes a mystery or suspense subplot constitutes romantic suspense. In my mind, however, a romantic suspense mixes both genres fairly equally. One strand (romance or suspense) does not significantly overwhelm the other."

Roxanne St Claire, author, has written a good article with the title Unraveling the Complexities of Romantic Suspense. This is an in depth study of the genre and well worth reading. She says, in her opinion, "a romantic suspense is a novel with a story that is driven equally and simultaneously by the threat of danger and the promise of romance. There are as many variations on this *theme as there are types of writers - from hot, erotic love stories with a hint of danger to a cozy mystery with a mere allusion to a possible romance."*

Several other writers defined romantic suspense, but the general opinion is that it is a 50/50 split of the two genres. The other thing I noticed is that it seems to be a fairly new genre, and Mary Stewart is referred to as the first writer to adapt the gothic romance novel into romantic suspense, in the 1950s.

By this time, I felt I had a good enough handle on romantic suspense to commence my reading.

The first book I read in this genre was *The Gingerbread Man,* by Maggie Shayne, and it erased all my preconceptions of the mixture of romance with crime, in a crime novel. This book mixed child abduction and murder with an ongoing romantic story involving a cop, and a young woman whose sister had been abducted when both of them were children. Both strands of the plot worked well, weaving together in a satisfactory way. The action was breathtaking and the suspense built steadily to reach an exciting climax. Meanwhile the romance aspect of the story developed in time-honoured fashion from initial resentment and dislike to a growing attachment which both main characters resisted until their passions overcame them, and ended up with a satisfactory conclusion. I must say I am not in the habit of reading romantic fiction, so I did not expect to like this book as much as I did. However, the blend of romance and suspense pulled me in and I enjoyed it.

My next choice was *Silent Deceit*, by Kallie Lane. This was a novella set in Canada, so it was a shorter read, and it was completely different to the previous book. The crime element in this one involved a female undercover cop looking for her brother who is missing. The action is set in a bikers' bar and the boss of the bar is a real villain. I had mixed feelings about this one, and although it was well written I could not get into the characters. The villain was underdeveloped and only appeared on the scene fleetingly which I thought was a lost opportunity. Further development could have made him more menacing and intensified the suspense. The romance element seemed to be more of a sex element, and if you like your romance hot and steamy this may be the book for you. I thought it was disjointed, with the sex scenes added in between the action. It was not a book with the feel good factor, although you might feel differently. It just wasn't for me. I am not even sure it met the criteria of a romantic suspense book.

The next book I read was *Imposter*, by Karen Fenech, and I was hooked from the first chapter. This author certainly knows how to write suspense, and the beginning of the novel was extremely fast paced. After such an exciting start the rest of the book flowed and was well structured. It was expertly written and the characterization was excellent. If the initial fast pace had been maintained it would have made an uncomfortable read, but there were quieter passages, sexy passages, and more suspense passages, all expertly intermingled to make a well structured and satisfying novel.

I have noticed with romantic suspense books that they are sexier than other crime novels which is in no doubt due to the romance element, and this book was no exception. It was a woman in jeopardy novel, with the two main characters distrustful of each other, and fighting the sexual attraction they both felt. The romance and the suspense were so entwined it would be difficult to separate the plot strands, and I think that truly makes this a prime example of romantic suspense fiction.

When I started reading my selection of books in this genre, I do not think I had fully grasped how graphic the sexual scenes would be. I am not a prude, and I have written sex scenes in my time, but nothing quite as graphic as I found in these novels. In comparison to mainstream crime novels and the different subgenres, sex is not a taboo subject, but again, I have not come across anything quite as explicit as the sex scenes in romantic suspense. I can only assume this is the romance influence on the books, and readers of romance fiction are looking for something more graphic than crime writers provide.

Now, after I cool down, I will move on to the next subgenre of crime on my list – the historical crime novel.

11

The Historical Crime Novel

What is a historical crime novel? Is it a subgenre of crime fiction, or a subgenre of historical fiction? Or is it a combination of both?

Mike Ashley provides a detailed and thoroughly researched article in Barry Forshaw's *British Crime Writing: An Encyclopedia, Vol 1*. He covers a variety of different types of historical crime fiction, from the early stories by Melville Davisson Post in the United States, featuring Uncle Abner in nineteenth-century Virginia. Meanwhile, in Britain, Jeffery Farnol published *An Amateur Gentleman* in 1913, featuring Jasper Shrig, a Bow street Runner. He goes on to refer to Georgette Heyer, Baroness Orczy, Russell Thorndike, Robert Graves, Wilkie Collins, Peter Lovesey, Ellis Peters, and many others. More recent authors include David Wishart, Michael Jecks, C J Sansom, Gillian Linscott, Joan Lock, and Alanna Knight. There would seem to be a multitude of authors writing historical mysteries where *"the author has to create an authentic and believable historical world and convey the differences in culture and attitude to the reader while still producing a story accessible to the modern mind."*

Joyce Saricks indicates in *The Readers' Advisory Guide to Genre Fiction*, that historical fiction is a story set in the past. These novels rely on historical facts and details which includes setting, customs, beliefs, culture and society, as well as characters and events. She considers historical mysteries provide a shorter introduction to a particular period, giving the impression they are less detailed and more readable. In her comprehensive guide the authors Saricks makes reference to as writing in the historical mystery subgenre include, Anne Perry, Margaret Lawrence, and Lindsey Davis.

H.R.F. Keating in *Writing Crime Fiction* describes historical crime fiction as *"combining mystery with history"* and he classifies it as cosy crime as opposed to unsettling crime. This reinforces the belief that this subgenre is an easier read than other genres of fiction.

None of this answers my question, therefore I think it is up to the reader to determine why they are reading the book. Are they reading it because they like historical novels? Or do they just like a good crime story with the added flavour of being set in the past? I can read a historical novel for either of these reasons, and as well as reading a lot of crime I also enjoy reading history. You might be interested to know that, as well as my contemporary crime fiction, I have published historical crime, and a historical saga which has nothing whatsoever to do with crime.

So what do I like about historical crime fiction? Well, it is a great way to find out about the past providing the historical facts are accurate. But, I do not want to read a dry list of dates and events. Mixing it up with a crime and giving it a fictional story makes it more appealing, it is a history lesson on the sly. Besides, I have a deep interest in crime and criminals, and that includes the past and how things have changed over time. The only thing I ask for in a historical crime novel, is that it must be a good story and be historically accurate. My main interest, however, lies with how people lived rather than what king was on the throne, or what wars were being waged. I can do without the politics as long as the living details of the characters acting out the story are accurate.

As far as I am concerned, a historical mystery or crime story must be thoroughly researched, but the research should not be visible. I do not want the author to break off from telling the story in order to inform me of salient historical facts. I want the historical background to be interwoven with the story, so I can be transported to that time and place.

Writers of historical fiction tackle it in different ways. Some writers use modern style language while remaining factually accurate in their historical detail. David Wishart, who writes the Corvinus detective series springs to mind. He writes in the style of Raymond Chandler, and wisecracks his way through a world of murder in first century AD Rome, but he is meticulous in his research of historical facts.

Other writers use a grammatical style and vocabulary more suited to the period in which they are writing. While this style is probably accurate for their period I find these historicals somewhat tedious, and not particularly suited to the crime genre, although that is only my opinion, therefore, feel free to differ.

Author and creative writing tutor B.D. Logue says – *"This subgenre does just what it says on the tin transposing the action to the past. The story itself may be a thriller, spy story, detective, locked room or police procedural but the challenges in respect of research and authenticity remain the same."*

The first book I read in the historical crime genre was *Death of a Serpent*, by Susan Russo Anderson. It is set in Sicily in 1866, with a storyline of murdered prostitutes, disinterested police, an amateur sleuth, and a mysterious killer. This book fulfilled all the criteria of historical crime, but it could also have been classified as a cosy crime with a historical setting. There are no details of gore or violence in this book, nor is there any sex, even though the victims are prostitutes and much of the investigation takes place in a brothel. The amateur detective is a widowed midwife with seven children of her own, and she becomes involved with the investigation of the murders through her friendship with Rosa, the brothel madam. Serafina Florio, the amateur sleuth, made a good, if somewhat unusual investigator. And I did not guess the killer's identity until the author revealed it. The Sicilian backdrop was well depicted and added to the atmosphere of the story, and the descriptions were excellent. I enjoyed reading this.

I have never been particularly interested in reading about the Middle Ages, a period characterized mainly by the growth in power of monarchy and the church. However, I have read, and enjoyed, *Pillars of the Earth*, and *World Without End*, both of which are set in the Middle Ages, but this was because I like Ken Follett's books. So, these novels, which are historical fiction rather than historical crime, are the exception, and I would normally steer clear of books set during this period.

However, I wanted variation among my book choices which was why I chose a crime novel set in the fourteenth century. This was a time before forensics, crime detection theories, and police forces, and I was not sure what to expect from a story set in this period. When I started reading, it was with a feeling it might not be to my taste.

The book I chose was Dennis Hamley's *Of Dooms and Death*, and I must admit I did not know what a Doom was until I read this book. For the uninitiated, it is a painting that depicts the Last Judgement. The first third of the book reads like historical fiction, building character of Joslin de Lay a French minstrel who has come to England. This made me think the main focus was going to be historical fiction and the crime possibly an after thought. How wrong I was, because once the crime element appeared it became a really exciting read.

When I got the background details out of the way and Joslin arrives in Stovingham, he becomes embroiled in murder. He meets two artists who are creating the great Doom painting in the church. But each time the face of one of the damned is painted, the person whose portrait it is, meets a violent death, and Joslin, as the stranger in the town, is blamed. He narrowly escapes death, becomes hunted, and vows to unmask the killer.

Despite my initial reservations, I did enjoy this book. It was not a traditional crime story in the way I understand it, and I wonder if a better description might be – a historical crime thriller. I will certainly read the other books in the Joslin de Lay series.

The third book I read for this topic was *House of the Wicked*, by D M Mitchell. On his Amazon author page, his work is compared to a selection of writers including Dean Koontz, who is a favourite of mine. However, when I started reading I had mixed feelings. It was written in a gothic style, and the writing was more literary than mainstream. As a result I was unable to get into the characters. There was also an excessive use of the pronoun 'he' which led to some confusion between the characters. Further confusion in the storytelling was caused by the frequent use of flashbacks with no transition between the past and present (in story terms). However, the flashbacks were needed, particularly as the book developed, but I would have appreciated knowing when it was a flashback.

The first part of the book was quite slow, concentrating on the background to the story. It was only after I passed the halfway point I started to become gripped, and it turned into a page turner. Readers who like their historical fiction written in a historical style will probably find this book to their taste. However, if the reader finds the story slow to start, I would say persevere because the latter half of the book is an exciting read with an ending that surprised even me.

Despite the negatives for me in this book, there were also a lot of positives. Porthgarrow, the setting of the story, is a superstition ridden community. The people are suspicious of incomers and believe Baccan, a mythical creature, influences their lives. The story is atmospheric, and there is a real gothic feel to it as it fluctuates between crime and horror. I particularly liked the mystery surrounding the death of Jowan Connoch's mother, and the aftermath that had for her son. The author uses language and imagery well which contributes to the overall feeling of doom and gloom, and there was a pervading sense of mystery throughout the whole book, although that did not always lead to suspense in the writing.

On the whole, I am glad I stuck with this book mainly because of the increasing pace in the latter half, the mystery, and the unexpected ending. And interestingly, this last book was the one that stayed with me the longest after I had moved to other categories, which I found surprising, considering my reaction to it at the time.

My next choice was *Uneasy Spirits* by M. Louisa Locke. This was a book set in nineteenth century San Francisco, and it's main theme centres around the fascination people had for spiritualism at this time.

Annie Fuller, the main character, is a widow who runs a boarding house, and gives clairvoyant readings as Madam Sybil. She is skilled in giving financial and relationship advice, and the only way she can practise these skills is through Madam Sybil. She does not believe in spirtualism or the after life so when one of her boarders asks for her help to expose a married couple who prey on vulnerable people, one of whom is her sister, she embarks on an investigation of the couple.

The novel starts with a murder, but then diverts into an investigation of the fake mediums, so that, in a sense, the reader forgets about the murder until the final twists in the story. Annie is a fascinating character, an independent woman living at a time when there were many restrictions on women.

I liked this novel which was rooted in the historical period it portrayed. It was atmospheric with a sense of mystery, although slightly lacking in suspense due to the slower pace. The storyline reflected the passion of the times for the supernatural and the belief in life after death with descriptive passages of séances and the tricks mediums used to ensnare the participants. The role of women in society and the home was also explored, reflecting a time when women were less free.

There was something genteel about this book which I thought was a murder mystery, sidetracked by the psychic investigation, which led to a really good twist, and an exciting and unexpected ending. This was a very clever book.

In comparison to mainstream crime fiction, I thought these books measured up favourably. They were all exciting, the historical detail was accurate, and the puzzle element was sufficient to keep me guessing.

My next chapter deals with a category of crime fiction that is becoming increasingly popular – paranormal or supernatural crime novels, sometimes known as psychic crime fiction.

12

Paranormal/Supernatural Crime Fiction

I have always liked supernatural fiction, and have read more than my share of horror books, so when I came to look at supernatural crime it was with a certain amount of relish because this was mixing my two favourite fiction genres.

However, before going any further, I wanted a clear understanding of supernatural fiction. In the *Occult and Supernatural Literature* section of *The Oxford Companion to Crime & Mystery Writing*, Clive Bloom writes *"Supernatural fiction deals with occult forces or forces from a spiritual realm that break through into common reality. Such forces take shape as ghosts, spirits, demons, and fairies, and challenge rationalist and scientific assumptions. Inherent in these stories is the belief that the world of ordinary reality is surrounded by an often hostile, inexplicable, and powerful spiritual world."* This explains supernatural literature, but what about the crime element.

In the *Psychic Detectives* section of Barry Forshaw's *British Crime Writing: An Encyclopedia, Vol 2*, Kim Newman, who wrote the section, considers it to be cheating if the mystery is solved solely by supernatural means, stating that *"slate-writing, ouija-boards, mind-reading, spiritualistic séances, crystal-gazing, and the like, are taboo."* The reader must be allowed to match his or her wits with the detective on an even playing field. He refers to S S Van Dine's twenty rules for writing detective stories which were published in the *American Magazine* in September 1928. Rule 1 states that *"The reader* must have equal opportunity with the detective for solving the mystery. All clues must be plainly stated and described." and rule 8 states that the crime must be solved by naturalistic means without resort to spiritualistic means.

There has been an upsurge of supernatural fiction over recent years, probably arising from the popularity of *Buffy the Vampire Slayer* and *Twilight*. But there is a much longer history of supernatural fiction, and I am sure everyone has heard of Bram Stoker's *Dracula*, published in 1897. There were also authors combining crime and the supernatural during this period. Sheridan Le Fanu published his first novel T*he Cock and Anchor* in 1845, and Algernon Blackwood introduced Dr John Silence, who investigates supernatural crimes, in *Dr John Silence, Physician Extraordinary*, which was published in 1908. They were not the only authors writing supernatural crime at this time, but the genre changed slightly over the following years, and writers such as Arthur Conan Doyle, and John Dickson Carr were presenting more rational explanations for supernatural crime stories.

More recently there has been a resurgence of the supernatural element, with Tony Hillerman's stories about the Navajo, and Clive Bloom says about his books, *"The matter-of-fact way the dimension of the spirit world is presented and accepted contrasts with Doyle's and Carr's debunking and makes a legitimate place again for the supernatural in detective fiction."*

Following on from this, the crime writer, Christopher Fowler says, *"Crime and the supernatural are a marriage made in heaven – and hell,"* and for me that sounds about right.

Supernatural or, if you prefer, occult crime fiction is not a new subgenre. You only have to think of Bram Stoker's classic novel *Dracula* to understand that, or Sheridan le Fanu's occult detective, Dr Martin Hesselius. Dennis Wheatley was another favourite of mine. He wrote many books, but I liked his black magic ones, including *The Devil Rides Out*, and *The Ka of Gifford Hillary*. He wrote eight books in this series which were bestsellers in the 1960s and 70s. However, they have now fallen out of fashion because of their satanic themes and instances of sadism. Another more recent favourite is John Connolly with his Charlie Parker series. He mixes a blend of the supernatural and crime in his extremely popular books.

Some of the better known detectives featured in paranormal or supernatural crime fiction include Dirk Gently, the detective in *Dirk Gently's Holistic Detective Agency*, by Douglas Adams, the renowned writer of *The Hitch Hikers Guide to the Galaxy*. Another of my favourites is the *Disc World* series by Terry Pratchett, which often features Captain Samuel Vimes.

So, a marriage of crime and fantasy, whether it is paranormal or supernatural, ticked all my boxes. But how do we determine whether the book is truly a crime book, or whether the fantasy supersedes it.

Studying my booklist, the first book I chose to read was *Eye of the Witch*, by Dana Donovan. I was drawn to the witch element in this book because I have studied and written articles on witchcraft. I have also written monologues and street theatre on the Forfar witches. However, I must admit all of this was in the historical sense rather than the modern.

At first, the book seemed to be a traditional detective story, and the paranormal elements were slow to make an appearance. Lilith, the witch, did not seem to play a dominant part until near the end of the book, and the main focus was on the detectives trying to solve suicides which they thought were murders. However, these murders were 'locked room' murders, and this is where the paranormal elements came in.

The paranormal elements the story included were clairvoyance, mental telepathy, bilocation and telekinesis. The book has characters who have 'out of body experiences' and one with a permanent metaphysical co-possession – two people in one body.

I was unsure about this book. It was well written, the investigation followed traditional lines with hints of the paranormal and witchcraft thrown in, but the solution of the crime would not have been possible without some of these paranormal happenings. So it did meet the criteria of a paranormal crime novel, although I could not help thinking that if the paranormal aspect had not been there, I would have thought the solution a cheat.

The next book I chose was not on my reading list, but I read about it on the Indie e-book Review site and this drew me to it. It was called *The Frankenstein Inheritance*, written by Simon Cheshire. As I have said before, I have always liked horror stories, and the review described the book as a 'gothic thriller' set in Jack the Ripper country, so it seemed to fit my supernatural crime category. And, as a lover of horror, how could I resist it.

The story concerns two children, Victoria and Albert, rescued from their creator Wolfgang von Frankenstein, by Professor Marchbanks who takes them to London. Frankenstein, of course, wants his creations whom he calls his children, returned to him. In the process of hunting them down, grisly murders are committed, and an army of the walking dead are on the children's trail.

Crimes are certainly committed in this novel, but I would say it was a horror story that includes crime, rather than the other way round. So, in a sense, it did not fit with my criteria, but it was a good read.

Back to my reading list – the next one I read was a cracker. It was *A Sorcerer Slain*, by Dave Sivers which genuinely fulfilled the criteria of a crime story with a fantasy setting.

This was a detective mystery that was also full of action and suspense, and it was a page-turner I could not put down. Lowmar Dashiel (nice name for a detective, I thought) is an inquisitor. He is tasked, by the King of Balimar, to find out who has murdered the Sorcerer Supreme. The problem is the chief suspect, Zarna, is heir to the Sorcerer General, and Dashiel is in love with her. As in all good mysteries and detective stories, Dashiel follows the clues, investigates the past life of the victim and comes up with an interesting solution to the crime. In the process of his quest (all good fantasy books have a quest), he meets many dangers and threats to his life, and someone is using magic to prevent him finding out the truth. I am not going to tell you any more as I would not want to spoil it for you, but this book certainly deserved the five stars I gave it when I finished reading, and I do not lightly award five stars to books unless they are exceptional.

I chose *Roman Dalton – Werewolf PI* by Paul D Brazill because it sounded different, and it was a good fit for the paranormal/supernatural section of this book. Besides, vampires and werewolves seem to be popular at the moment, probably because of the *Twilight* series, and several other books and television programmes featuring them. A werewolf private investigator is certainly unusual in crime fiction, and I wondered how the writer would handle the subject and how the story would develop.

After I started reading I realized that the book was an anthology of short stories, but because the main character featured in almost all of the stories, it had a continuity that many anthologies lack.

It did not take me long to discover that the title might be a misnomer, because Roman Dalton, acted more like a vigilante than a detective. This character, an ex-cop of twenty years, became a werewolf following an investigation which led to the attack that instigated the change. Forced to retire from the police force he became a private detective, although he did not seem to be involved in the usual type of private eye activity we have come to expect.

As a vigilante he hunts down evil doers and disposes of them werewolf fashion. He does not attack innocent people, although I did not find many of them in any of the stories. The settings were bleak, and the book had a post apocalyptic feel. It did not feel like the world we know, and there was a sense of doom and despair running through the book.

What I did like about this book was the language. It was written in a hard-boiled style, reminiscent of Spillane or Hammett. Phrases like *"the oil slick of the night was melting into a granite grey day,"* and *"Duffy's face was so acne-scarred it looked like a chewed up toffee apple,"* as well as *"a voice as dark and thick as the smoke from a french cigarette."* It was descriptive writing such as this that lifted the book out of the ordinary and made it something special.

This book may not be for everyone, but I do feel it was original, well written, and far better than much paranormal fiction currently on sale.

My next choice was *The Sleeping Warrior* by Sara Bain. This is a clever, well written book with an intricate plot. There are police procedural threads, fantasy threads, mysterious characters, illicit romance, and a serial killer who kills in a particularly nasty way.

After a narrow escape from a serial killer, the main character, solicitor Libby Butler, becomes involved with the mysterious Gabriel Radley, the sleeping warrior of the plot. He is hunting for a mysterious stone which he needs to enable him to take the creepy and repulsive Shinar back home in chains. Shinar is obviously evil personified, but Gabriel is an enigma and the reader is never entirely sure about him.

Shinar refers to Gabriel as a Vascaran, but everything else about the two men is a mystery; where they come from; who they are; why Gabriel is hunting Shinar; and why the stone is so important. These mysteries are never fully answered, although it is apparent both men are not of this world.

Alongside the main theme of the quest for the stone, runs the serial killer theme. A killer so depraved he drains his victims of blood and then dismembers them, and is nicknamed Dracula or the Vampire Killer by the media. Another theme involves the female contract killer, Rose Red, who disposes of people for a price; the gangster, and his Norwegian bodyguard, who are trying to trace a man hiding in a police-protected safe house, in order to acquire and dispose of a book manuscript; and a mysterious cult, The Awakening, composed of young savages who file their teeth and paint their faces red.

Initially all the disparate themes seemed to have no connection, but the threads of the plot were woven together with such skill they all came together in a logical fashion, and created such an atmosphere of suspense it made the book a page turner. This is certainly a book that would compare favourably with many books published traditionally.

The books in this chapter were all well written, and I enjoyed reading them. As far as a comparison with books published by mainstream publishers are concerned, I think they fare well and I would not hesitate to urge you to try some indie authors as well as the authors who are traditionally published.

Moving from the psychic to the psychological, my next chapter deals with psychological crime fiction – the whydunit.

13

Psychological Crime – The Whydunit

Crime fiction comes in many forms. However, when it originally became popular, it was with whodunits. These were the detective mysteries prevalent in the golden age. In the traditional whodunit, the plot is concerned with establishing the identity of the criminal. The whydunit, in contrast, is more concerned with finding out why the crime was committed, and in many of these stories the identity of the criminal is known at the beginning of the book. In others, where the identity of the perpetrator is not revealed at an early stage, the story may revolve around the psychological profile the investigator compiles.

On the other hand, Joyce Saricks refuses to categorize psychological fiction as being either linked to the crime or thriller genre. In her reference book *The Readers' Advisory Guide to Genre Fiction,* she says, *"If ever there were a group of books that is neither fish nor fowl, this is surely it. Called Suspense, Thrillers, Horror, Mystery, and sometimes just Psychological Fiction, these are genre orphans."* I tend to disagree. Surely a novel where psychology is the driving force as well as murder, and the investigation of that murder by the police, profilers, or detectives, has to be either psychological crime or mystery.

Louise Conley Jones in *The Oxford Companion to Crime & Mystery Writing* states that *"the detective in the whodunit seeks to establish material motive for the crime, the sleuth in the whydunit explores the psychological motivation that drives a person to perpetrate a crime."* This results in the whydunit being the most character driven subgenre in crime fiction.

I did find it strange that Barry Forshaw's *British Crime Writing: An Encyclopedia* had no section on psychological crime, or even the whydunit, considering the growing popularity of the genre. In recent years many books have been published featuring profilers using psychology to detect the criminal. Serial killers and mass murderers are frequently the characters used to populate these books, and it is a race against time to prevent the body count from mounting. Authors who use criminal profilers in their fiction include Patricia Cornwell, and Val McDermid.

It is safe to say that over the years crime fiction has grown and developed and now includes the whydunit as well as the whodunit. However, nothing is clear cut and many contemporary crime stories have elements of both. In fact, this is the way I write my crime fiction, merging the whodunit with the whydunit.

I have long been a fan of psychological crime, and I have read most of the big name authors who write in this genre. Authors such as Barbara Vine, Patricia Highsmith, Minette Walters, Thomas Harris, Mo Hayder, and Nicci French. So I came to this part of my booklist with considerable enthusiasm, and wondered how the independent authors fared compared to their more famous peers. However, I had some difficulty identifying suitable novels in this subgenre. Many of the novels which came up in a psychological crime fiction search seemed to be more psychic than psychological. And many of them would have been a better fit in the subgenre I discussed in my previous chapter, paranormal or supernatural crime.

The first book on my list was *Slow Burning Lies,* by Ray Kingfisher, who is a British author despite the book being set in Chicago. This was an intriguing story about a man who is experiencing extreme nightmares, which are becoming increasingly violent. Initially, I had my doubts because the story seemed to focus entirely on the nightmares. But when it developed beyond the nightmares, and his search for the reasons behind his experiences, the story developed momentum and certainly kept me guessing.

His narrative style was one I am not particularly fond of. Kingfisher has the narrator walking into a coffee shop and telling the waitress his story. So the narrator is in control all the way through. However, this was done with such skill I soon forgot the narrator and simply followed the story. The author was also skilled in his use of language, and I especially liked the phrase *"A foot appeared as if the wind had dropped it there."* And, of course, as well as suspense and all the other factors that keep a reader engrossed, is the mystery of the narrator's identity. Why is he telling a waitress his story? I am positive you will not guess the reason.

The next book I read was *Max,* by D M Mitchell, which was described as *"a psychological thriller combining mystery, crime and suspense"* so this seemed to fit in with my criteria of psychological crime. It was an intriguing book which did have elements of crime in it in the form of several murders, but these murders seemed to be more incidental than the real focus of the novel. It certainly had mystery and, although I thought I had figured the story out, the twist at the end was unexpected. However, it did not fit into anything that resembled a traditional crime story, although I think Barbara Vine sometimes writes in a similar way. What it did have was an intriguing psychological study of the main character. This novel was well written, although I found the structure somewhat unusual, and I am not too sure it was to my taste. On the other hand, of the books I read, this was the one that remained longest in my mind.

I was looking forward to my next selection, *Somewhere to*

Hide, by Mel Sherratt. It was described as the first book in a crime and psychological suspense series, with a recommendation by Mandasue Heller. However, once I started reading, it was not what I expected it to be. Maybe the description and recommendation meant my expectations were too high, or maybe the description was somewhat amiss. The book seemed to me to be more of a novel dealing with social issues, rather than a psychological crime novel. Admittedly there was crime in it including murder, as well as a smattering of psychology, but these took second place to the social issues the book dealt with.

Although the book did not meet my expectations it was well written, and it had a good plot which centred around Cathy who takes in waifs and strays. The social issues were handled well, although I felt my own background of social work intruded into my interpretation of the story. And of course this was my fault, not the author's.

I chose *The Baptist* by R.A. Barnes with the intention of including it in my serial killer crime section. However, once I started reading I soon realised that this was no ordinary serial killer story. Instead it was a psychological thriller of the highest order.

The plot was well structured and there was a lot of mystery around. The main character John, who thinks of himself as The Baptist, is a man with serious mental health problems. At the age of 14 he drowns his 11 year old brother Ray, in the bath. His motive for doing this is to save Ray from turning into his father. John spends the next 10 years in a mental institution where he meets another inmate Mary Crossan. He is eventually released into the community where he marries and fathers two daughters. For eight years he appears to be stable but then stops taking his medication. From then on his mental condition is on a downward spiral.

The story follows John during this period of mental deterioration. He leaves his wife and children, and meets Mary again. Mary is also seriously disturbed, seeming to have dual personality where she flips between being Mary and her other persona, Alice. The couple embark on a murderous journey and there are many bodies along the way. John fulfils his Baptist role by drowning his victims. Mary/Alice uses more bloody methods.

The fascination of this book is that it portrays the thinking of the two mentally disturbed characters. It gives the reader an insight into their delusional thinking, how their minds work, and how mentally disturbed they are. Despite that John is a likeable character and is able to gain the sympathy of the readers.

The book was well written, well plotted, and well structured. The writing was descriptive with plenty of suspense and mystery. This book would certainly compare well with any mainstream published book.

I came across the next book after picking up a postcard at Crimefest, the annual crime writing convention held in Bristol. The description indicated it met the criteria of a psychological crime novel, so I bought the e-book.

The novel was *Secrets Only Sleep*, by Barbara Fagan Speake. This was an excellent psychological crime thriller, combined with a relationship thread to the plot. Michael, a security expert, combines forces with the recently widowed Christine, to solve the murder of a bag lady. The novel abounds with mystery, as well as an insight into the inner lives of all the main characters which makes it an intriguing read. Apart from this the characters are well drawn, and I genuinely cared about them. The story follows the investigation into the mystery of the bag lady's murder as well as the burgeoning relationship between Michael and Christine. The suspense is maintained throughout and culminates in a thrilling way that had me holding my breath.

This is a book that fulfilled all my expectations of a psychological crime novel, although it could equally fit the mystery, and the romantic suspense subgenres. I would have no hesitation in recommending this book, it was excellent. I will be looking out for more books written by this author.

The books I read for this section differed greatly in their content and plotting, but they were all well written, and engaged my interest. Again I am not sure how they match up to their more famous counterparts who publish in the traditional way. But it is inherently unfair to compare them to authors who are bestsellers and at the top of their game. All I can say is that these indie authors are a match for many of the traditionally published crime novels which grace a bookstore's shelves.

Humour is not something many readers associate with crime fiction, but it exists and can often be a satisfying and pleasurable read. If you have never read a funny crime novel then move on to the next chapter where I will introduce you to funny side of crime.

14

Humour and Crime: A Strange Mix

Whether your taste in crime fiction is a cosy, or a good police procedural, there is no doubt in my mind that crime fiction over the years has become progressively darker. So, what place does humour play in a genre based on mystery and murder? Surely crime and humour make uneasy bedfellows.

After all, writers use humour in fiction to make the reader laugh. Humorous scenes paint the funny, incongruous, or ludicrous, in people and events. But crime is a serious matter involving misery and death.

The reference books on crime fiction do not have much to say about humour in the crime novel. One of the reasons for its low profile may be that, according to Lesley Grant-Adamson in *Writing Crime Fiction*, humorous writing is regarded as more difficult to sell. I always thought the opposite, but publishers are the gatekeepers when it comes to supplying the book reading market, therefore there could be a supply problem. I am sure many indie writers will be more than willing to fill this gap. The traditional crime authors who use humour in their novels include: Simon Brett, Christopher Brookmyre, Lindsay Davis, Carl Hiasson, and David Wishart.

I must admit most of my crime reading is firmly placed in the dark or noir type of crime fiction. However, I do like Christopher Brookmyre's earlier novels, which are not only dark, but excruciatingly funny. So, in my quest for well written indie e-books which tell satisfying stories, I simply had to include humour, although I am not even sure what humour consists of in a crime novel.

Black humour is, of course, the obvious one, followed closely by satire. Then there are the spoof ones, rather like the airplane films which Leslie Nielsen did so well. And I suppose I should include the humour raised in the interplay between some double acts, Holmes and Watson spring to mind. Then there is the gentle humour displayed by Agatha Christie's, Miss Marple, as well as Dorothy L Sayers, with Lord Peter Wimsey. I also find some crime television series excellent at combining crime with humour. Two of my favourites are *Rizzoli and Isles*, and *Castle*, although I read one of the spin off Nikki Heat books from the *Castle* series, and I was not impressed.

Now, before I compiled my list and started reading, I had to admit to myself that I do not possess a funny bone. Humorous writing, which has my friends doubled up with laughter, often does not raise a smile with me. So, when I talk about the books I have read, please bear this in mind.

The first book I chose was *The Sparrow Conundrum*, by Bill Kirton. I have read Bill Kirton's excellent dark crime books before and knew I liked his writing style. But this book was the winner of the humour category in the 2011 Forward National Literature Awards, and has recently won The Readers' Choice Award, so I reckoned it could fit my criteria of a humorous crime novel.

After a brief period of confusion, which was not surprising, considering this is a spoof crime novel, I started chuckling and then laughing. I think I became as manic as the book. It is a story full of surprises, twists and turns. The characters are over the top, from the weak-kneed Machin to the psychotic police inspector who is constantly trying to rearrange evidence to increase his arrest and conviction figures, and who has it in for Machin. Mysterious figures come and go and get up to all kinds of shenanigans. I especially liked Mary, with her/his moustache and large frame, who kept popping up at regular intervals. I won't say anymore about the characters or plot because I do not want to spoil it for new readers. But, be assured if you start reading this you, will be entertained from beginning to end, and if it made me laugh out loud then I am sure it will make you laugh.

The next book on my list was *Cross Dressed to Kill*, by Andrew Lucas. This book apparently won the CGD Easy Reading Award in 2011, and although I am not familiar with this award it made the book sound promising. The story is about a likeable camp hairdresser who looks on his murders as a series of misfortunes. He starts off on his murderous trail, when one of his customers annoys him so much, he 'accidentally' disposes of her. From there he embarks on a trail of further murders, which as the book progresses, become more planned and deliberate. The situations he gets himself into provide much of the humour as he lurches from one crisis to the next.

This book has been described as British black humour at its best. The book is certainly British, and the humour is certainly black, although I think, on balance, Christopher Brookmyre does it better. However, this was an entertaining read, and I came away thinking it would also have been a good fit with my psychological crime book choices, as well as my, yet to come, serial killer book choices.

For my third choice of humorous crime, I selected *Never Buried*, by Edie Claire, and I must say I thoroughly enjoyed reading this. It is the story of Leigh Koslow an out of work copywriter, and her two friends, Maura, a somewhat large policewoman, and Cara, her pregnant cousin. There is also a rather vicious, badly behaved cat called Mao Tse. Leigh and Cara discover a body in the hammock in their garden, and that is the beginning of a rather good mystery because the body is at least ten years old, and there is no indication of where it has been, its identity, or who dumped it there.

The humour in this novel is generated by the characters and their interplay with each other, and it gives the story a light and breezy feel, as well as making it easy to read. This also put it firmly in the cosy category of crime fiction, although it had a terrific suspenseful ending.

This chapter has dealt with humour in crime. All three books were enjoyable, all very different, and all featuring differences in the humour used in the writing. This has made the reading particularly enjoyable.

And now to move on to something quite different, the medical crime thriller.

15

The Medical Crime Thriller

The crimes in a medical thriller usually take place in a medical setting. It may be a hospital, a medical centre, a research establishment, or a forensics lab. The main characters have a medical or research background, and become heavily involved in detecting the crime that has been committed.

A medical setting is nothing new in crime fiction, and novels with a medical theme have been around since the start of the twentieth century. R Austin Freeman introduced his scientific sleuth, Dr John Thorndyke, in *The Red Thumb Mark,* published in 1907. Ngaio Marsh and P.D. James have used nursing homes as settings for their books. P.D. James has also used a psychiatric clinic, and a training college for nurses in her novels. The best known medical thriller writer is, of course, the American author Robin Cook. All these writers used medical settings in what you might call a traditional way, using the settings as closed communities, although the medical themes are wider ranging, addressing moral and ethical issues alongside conspiracy themes and murder.

Similar to all other crime thrillers, the medical crime thriller continues to develop. The advance of forensics in solving crimes has brought forward authors exploiting new developments in the field. Patricia Cornwell, introduced her forensic pathologist character, Kay Scarpetta, in *Post Mortem* in 1990, the first book of a successful series. Kathy Reichs published *Deja Dead* in 1997, featuring Tempe Brennan, a forensic anthropologist. And British author, Val McDermid has published a series of novels featuring her psychologist character, Dr Tony Hill. Another favourite of mine is American author Jonathan Kellerman who created Dr Alex Delaware, a child psychologist and police consultant.

My own preferences in medical crime thrillers are the ones where murder is the main theme. I am less fond of the conspiracy thrillers where science and medicine come together to overthrow governments or countries. So my choice of medical thriller may not be your choice, and my likes and dislikes about the books I read may vary greatly from that of other readers.

For my first choice of book, I chose one written by Ken McClure, an award winning medical scientist who has been traditionally published but is now publishing his back list independently, so he meets the criteria of an indie author. According to his bio on Amazon, he has written twenty-three novels, so I thought I could not go far wrong by reading one of his books for this project. The book I chose was *Past Lives,* which is described as a medical thriller exploring multiple personality disorder. I had previously read books about this condition, and my understanding was MPD is a condition where more than one person inhabits the same body, and the person may be controlled by any of the other personalities without their knowledge. However, the interpretation of MPD in this thriller, while basically the same, involved the other personalities being exposed through drugs, and emerging as personalities from the past, which seemed to me to be a theme of reincarnation. I suppose the clue was in the title of the book *Past Lives.*

The main character in the novel is an American neurosurgeon, John Macandrew who becomes involved in trying to uncover the mystery of why one of his patients became someone else after brain surgery. In attempting to solve the mystery he travels to Scotland and Paris, becomes involved with

Simone Robin, a molecular biologist, and both of them try to prevent the priest, Dom Ignatius, obtaining new supplies of the serum he needs to make his patient undergo the transformation into a past life. Needless to say the main characters face many dangers and risk their lives in the process.

The chase and capture scenes reflected a slight similarity to one of Dan Brown's novels, and the serum altering personality injections seemed to have a hint of Jekyll and Hyde. The settings galloped between Kansas, Scotland, Paris and Malta, and the pace of the novel was quite fast. It was a satisfying read, although there were some minor editing and proofing glitches which did not get in the way of the reading and enjoyment of the book.

I chose the second book *The Operator* by Valerie Laws because I had been impressed by her first crime novel, *The Rotting Spot*, which I use in a later section of this book, under Noir/Dark Crime Fiction. As the Medical Crime Thriller is an addition to the original e-book festival blog posts, which were written earlier, this second book had not yet been published when I commented on *The Rotting Spot*. I finished off my comment on this first book with 'I will be looking out for more books by this author', so when *The Operator* was published I had to read it.

The Operator is the name given to a serial killer who is murdering surgeons in a particularly gruesome way, and Erica Bruce, an amateur sleuth, becomes embroiled in the investigation when she discovers the body of the first victim. It is not long before she is crossing swords with Inspector Will Bennett, and their love/hate relationship ensures plenty of sparks will fly.

The Geordie speaking Stacy, who was in the first book, reappears in this one as well, providing a much needed blast of humour to the proceedings. The romantic element is supplied by

Erica's burgeoning relationship with a young, half-chinese doctor, and their increasingly sexual encounters, which displeases Will Bennett.

Erica pursues the investigation in a dogged fashion and continually gets up the nose of Will Bennett and the police investigating team. There are loads of twists and turns along the way, with the final one being a complete surprise. The climax of the book is bound to set pulses racing, as it gallops to the end at breakneck speed.

This second crime novel by Valerie Laws was every bit as good as her first one, and I hope she continues to write crime because she is a talented crime writer.

I struggled with my next book choice. The medical detail was spot on, but I found it far too slow with too many characters and strands, as well as technical detail. There were good bits in it but by the time I was at the half-way mark I still wasn't sure where the plot was going, or even what the plot was. I am sure the story would have developed if I had stuck with it, and it might have had more appeal to dedicated medical crime thriller readers, but it was not to my taste so I stopped reading to concentrate on something more to my liking.

I like forensic thrillers. I have read Cornwell, Reichs, and McDermid for years, so I thought I would try a forensic thriller for my third choice, although I doubted any other author, indie or traditional, would match up to the aforementioned authors who are all at the top of their game.

Nothing daunted, I downloaded *Evidence of Malice: Book One*, by Kim M Allen. I was unable to find out anything about the author. No website, and nothing on the author Amazon page, and it appeared to be a first book despite having Book One as part of the title. However, the reviews were good, and several were Amazon verified purchases, plus I have always been drawn to first books whether traditionally or indie published.

It was quite a short book (82 pages) and it was a fast read. I started and finished reading the same day. So what can I say. It was a great plot, well paced, and held the interest. The writing was taut, although this meant the characters were not as well developed as they could have been, although they were by no means cardboard characters. I did find the forensic detail less than convincing, although the average reader might not have a problem with this. For example, the lead forensic investigator is a jack of all trades. He leads his team of forensic techies, he dusts for fingerprints and carries out other forensic tasks, as well as performing autopsies on the bodies. Now, normally a forensic investigator is a scientist, and the person doing the autopsy is a medical pathologist, two entirely different professions. Not unless things are done differently in America, of course. Not only that, he tells the police the killer is a serial killer, despite only one body having been found at the time he makes this pronouncement, and he gives a specific time of death, to the minute, after a few minutes of seeing the body. Dental records are matched within the hour, enabling him to identify the body, and autopsies are performed in the forensics lab rather than the mortuary or morgue. There were some graphic scenes of violence in this book, as well as sexual scenes, and a thrilling denouement.

Despite the forensic failings I did enjoy the book. I felt it was a cracking good story and I would read this author again.

It is time to move on again, and I will be looking at the legal crime thriller, or legal procedural as it is otherwise known, in the next chapter.

16
The Legal Crime Thriller

Crime fiction and thrillers with a focus on the law, the legal professions, and the dispensing of justice, which are also known as legal procedurals, have become increasingly popular since John Grisham published his first novel *A Time to Kill*, in 1989. However, the legal thriller is not a new form. Like a lot of crime fiction it has its roots in the past, as far back as the 1500s with George Harsdorffer's *A Gallery of Horrible Tales of Murder*, and Matthias Abele von und zu Lilienberg's *Metamorphosis and Unusual Law Cases*. And, of course, the *Newgate Calendars* published between 1734 to 1828.

Since then many authors have written and published legal crime thrillers. Among them are Erle Stanley Gardner, John Mortimer, Scott Turow, Frances Fyfield, Steve Martini, and many more, not forgetting the previously mentioned John Grisham who has contributed greatly to the genre's ongoing popularity.

The definition of a legal procedural given by Jon L. Breen, in *The Oxford Companion to Crime & Mystery Writing* is given as: *"A type of novel that shows lawyers engaged in the business of law. It is likely to have a lawyer as detective and at some stage may take the reader into a courtroom. At its best, it will turn on a specific point of law."*

That seems clear enough, but it made me wonder whether I could find stories in the indie books to match those of the traditional authors, like John Grisham, Steve Martini, and Scott Turow. And would there be characters to match those of Erle

Stanley Gardner's Perry Mason, or John Mortimer's Horace Rumpole of the Bailey, or even Frances Fyfield's Helen West. I am aiming high.

For my first choice I thought I would do something different, and instead of just commenting on the book I read, I would include the full review which I did for the Famous Five Plus website after winning the book on their site. I hadn't read any books by this author before, but this legal thriller really impressed me. It is *A Fatal Verdict*, written by Tim Vicary.

"I am an avid crime reader but must admit I do not normally read court-room dramas. I am not sure why this is, maybe it is because I cannot get rid of the feeling that because the setting is a formal one, this will detract from the suspense of the story. However, I won this book in a competition, so it follows that I had to read it. Well, I am glad I did, because this was one of the most thrilling, page-turners I have read for some time.

The characters were realistic, and I was completely drawn in by Sarah Newby, who was no formal, dry as dust QC. She was a living, breathing character with her own family problems, and dilemmas. She dispelled the image of wig and gown, although she did wear them in court, but she also travelled to court on her high-powered motor bike, and when she was angry she revved the bike and drove dangerously at high speed.

The book starts with the discovery of the body of a young girl in the bath of her boyfriend's flat. She is partially drowned and has slit wrists. It soon transpires that she hasn't committed suicide, she has been murdered, with her boyfriend the main suspect. Sarah has the job of prosecuting him, and the resultant court case is full of suspense.

The girl's family are destroyed by her death, and when the boyfriend is killed they become the prime suspects, and Sarah has the job of defending the mother who is charged with the murder.

It has to be said that the identity of each murderer is never in doubt, but the events leading from these murders provide enough suspense to satisfy the most dedicated crime reader.

This was the second book in the Sarah Newby series but it is not necessary to read them in order as this book did well as a stand-alone crime story. Needless to say I'll now read the first book in the series, although I'll have to buy that one, as it would be a fluke if I won that one in a competition as well."

As you can see by the review of *A Fatal Verdict*, this was a book that measured up to my expectations about what a good read should be. So, now I am wondering if my next choices will be as good.

My luck was in because the next book I read, *Irreparable Harm*, by Melissa F Miller, was a page turner. The main character, Sasha McCandless, is an eighth year associate attorney with Prescott and Talbot, a large legal firm with over eight hundred lawyers. It was evident from the start that the author knew what she was writing about. I was curious about her experience and checked out her web site, and I found out that the author is a litigator, the same as her main character, Sasha, which explained the ease with which she described life in a legal firm. However, although there are some similarities between the author and her character, Sasha is definitely fictional. The author describes Sasha as *"single, childless, under five feet tall, under one hundred pounds, and could kill you with her bare hands."*

I found Sasha a fascinating character, and the reason she is so deadly is because she is a student of Krav Maga, a form of martial arts I had never heard of until I read this book. The only problem I had with her expertise in this field was that she was never at any serious risk from her opponents, so I didn't worry about her.

Sasha is appointed as the leader of a team of attorneys to

handle legal claims following an air-crash and develops suspicions there might be a conspiracy to crash commercial planes by remote control. She becomes involved with a Federal Air Marshall who is investigating a security leak of sensitive information. After one of Sasha's contacts is murdered, the two of them embark on a roller coaster of an adventure. A character with less martial arts experience would have been deemed to be at serious life risk during the course of the novel, but in my head I knew Sasha was more than a match for any killer who came after her.

Despite the fact that much of this novel was set in a corporate setting, this was no dry statement of fact. The descriptions and characters populating the offices of Prescott and Talbot were lively and interesting, the action was furious, the pace was fast, and there was an interesting mystery. If I had a criticism, it would be that the baddie at the end, spilled the beans too readily. It was a bit like an Agatha Christie denouement which says – this is what it was all about. But I really liked this book, and I think it is every bit as good as any traditionally published novel.

Now it is time to start reading legal thriller number three. Fingers crossed that this will be a good read as well.

The Good Lawyer, by Thomas Benigno, was my third choice. This book had good reviews, and it was written by a practising attorney who also had a great deal of experience working with Legal Aid cases, so I reckoned he had the background and legal experience to write a legal thriller.

The main character of this book is Nick Mannino, a Legal Aid lawyer who defends the people no one else wants to defend – the rapists, sexual abusers and drug dealers. I went back and looked at the bio of Thomas Benigno on the Amazon book page of *The Good Lawyer*, and it dawned on me that this book, although written as a fictional story, was in many ways autobiographical. The book itself is well written, and the legal details are authentic and accurate, however, I felt it slow to start and it seemed to be more of a story about the lawyer rather than a plot driven fictional novel.

I felt there was too much back story in the the first part of the book, and this slowed down the action. It lacked pace and suspense, and I was having difficulty identifying the story arc. I had resigned myself to following the lawyer's story which was quite interesting, when all of a sudden the book picked up and started to race. The suspense increased and the pace quickened and it became a really good story. The final scenes were exciting and intense, with one or two surprises linked to one of the back stories.

On the whole, despite the slow start, this was a good read, well written by an author who knew his subject.

Political crime is all around us. We may not recognize it, but it is there. There is the overarching politics of ruling governments, or the more subtle politics of the workplace. In the next chapter I will be attempting to find out how crime fiction handles this subject.

17

The Political Crime Thriller

In my search for definitions of a political crime thriller the emphasis seemed to be on thriller; the examples of crime fiction in this genre incorporated social issues, turning it into a socio-political genre. Not only that, but the emphasis was more on the social issues rather than the political ones.

Most of the examples of socio-political crime fiction in *The Oxford Companion to Crime & Mystery Writing* reflect this bias. This reference book quotes Robert Greene's *The Art of Coney Catching* (1591), as the the beginning of crime fiction's social concerns. This early novel is about the criminal world of 'coney-catchers' or con artists, and had themes of greed, lechery and Puritan hypocrisy. Others referred to are Charles Dickens's works, *Oliver Twist* (1837-39), and *Bleak House* (1853). Other examples of socio-political concerns in literature include the works of Arthur Conan-Doyle, Wilkie Collins, Agatha Christie, and Dorothy L Sayers. Among the American writers considered are Raymond Chandler, and Dashiell Hammett who expose corruption and degradation. In *Red Harvest*, (1929) Dashiell features *"corrupt city officials, cops on the take, striking miners, and rival mobsters of 'Poisonville',"* while in *The Glass Key* the theme is corrupt city politics.

The socio-political influence can also be seen in an upsurge of novels with ethnic detectives, such as Virgil Tibbs, an African American police detective, who first appeared in John Ball's acclaimed novel *In the Heat of the Night* (1985). Others include Martin Cruz Smith's gypsy detective, and Tony

Hillerman's Navajo tribal policeman. This is a small sample and there were many others. *The Oxford Companion to Crime & Mystery Writing* says that *"Each new ethnic detective has used new social and political perspectives on the genre, some decorative, some integral."*

Political thrillers may contain an element of crime, but this is not necessarily murder. Some of the themes in these novels are power, corruption, conspiracy, terrorism, and warfare. The backdrop is usually that of a political power struggle which can involve national or international political scenarios. There is a crossover between the political thriller and the spy thriller, often involving establishments like America's CIA, and Britain's MI6. Organizations such as the FBI and MI5 pull in the crime element, so that a political thriller can be considered crime fiction as well.

The evidence suggests that the political crime thriller incorporates social issues as well as political issues, and we only have to look at Charles Dickens, one of Britain's best known authors, to see how successful this could be. However, the type of political crime I am more interested in, when selecting my choice of reading examples, is corporate crime, government conspiracies, financial and fraudulent schemes, corruption, political terrorists, and all the different variations of this and how it ends up in murderous situations. So I am looking for murder, as well as political shenanigans.

Frederick Forsyth's *Day of the Jackal* is a good example of this type of book, with the Jackal on a murderous quest to assassinate the French president. David Baldacci is another author who writes about the abuse of power, particularly in his novel *Absolute Power*. Other authors who intersperse their adventure thrillers with crime thrillers include, Richard North Patterson, Sydney Sheldon, Michael Dobbs, and Lee Child.

The first book I read for this section was *Empty Places* by

Martin Roy Hill, and I chose it because one of the themes in its description was political corruption.

This was an American crime thriller as well as a murder mystery. It started with the shooting of an investigative reporter in the Californian desert, and the prologue featuring this scene was dramatic and stunning. I knew right from the beginning of the book it was going to be a good read.

The reporter's ex-husband, Peter, returns from the Honduras where he is a war correspondent, and accompanied by an ex-cop, embarks on an investigation to find her murderer.

As well as being a murder mystery, the book focuses on a variety of themes including drugs and porn. There are links to rebel groups such as the Contras and weapon smuggling, political themes and corruption, which illustrates the advantages corrupt entrepeneurs gain by political funding.

Although I chose this book for its political element this was not the main theme, and the novel focused more on crime and the murder mystery aspect. So this book satisfied the criteria of a good crime novel with some political content. However, it was a really good read, fast paced and exciting, with much descriptive writing of Palm Springs and the Californian desert regions.

My next choice was *The Loyal Servant* by Eva Hudson. This British book had everything – it was well written, well plotted, and met all the criteria of a political crime thriller. It had murder, conspiracy, misuse of power, and corruption that reached the highest level of the government.

The main character, Caroline Barber, makes an unusual amateur sleuth. She is middle-aged, with a husband, and three children, and she works as a civil servant in the Academies Division of the Department for Education. When she finds the Schools Minister's body slumped over his desk, she is the only one who does not believe he committed suicide and she is convinced he was murdered. She ferrets around trying to find evidence and teams up with Angela Tate, a newspaper reporter who is fighting against redundancy and early retirement. They follow a trail that becomes increasingly dangerous, and what started out as a cosy crime novel turns into an exciting thriller which keeps turning up the suspense until it reaches a chilling climax.

The storyline in this novel was well crafted and the characterization was excellent. As well as Caroline and Angela, there was a slimy security man, an unpleasant boss, well differentiated colleagues of both women, corrupt politicians, and a ruthless business woman. But the secondary character I liked the most, was Caroline's pensioner mother, Jean, a street fighting anarchist and protestor. These characters were real people, with real emotions and actions, and I was hooked from page one.

This book is a match for anything the traditional publishers produce, and is a good example of what indie books can offer the discerning reader.

Next I read *The Fellowship*, written by William Tyree, because I was attracted to its description as a political thriller. It included the murder of high ranking politicians in the US and the UK which made me think that it would fit nicely with my reading of indie books for this subgenre.

The book was well written, well plotted, and an intriguing story, but I found the structure somewhat unusual. It was written in four parts. Parts one and four were set in contemporary times and had everything you would expect from a political thriller. There were gruesome murders, thrilling action, conspiracy, religion, politics and mystery. The pace was frenetic and it was a page turner. However, parts two and three were set in the past, and the story became historical fiction. The pace in this part of the book was slower, although I found the historical background intriguing and interesting. I would, however, hesitate to say it was still a crime story or a thriller, unless we consider that nazism, a crime against humanity, satisfies the definition of crime used in this book. The research in the historical sections was impeccable, and I was fascinated by details of the Hitler youth, the SS, and Himmler's fixation on acquiring the art and artefacts of Europe for the Reich. The rise of the Fellowship, and the murderous Black Order was rooted in this section of the book, and as such supplied the motivation for the crimes in the contemporary section.

When I finished reading *The Fellowship* I was at a loss how to categorize it. It was partly crime, partly political thriller, and yet a major part of the book was straightforward historical fiction. All I can say is that I enjoyed reading it, even if at times the research showed.

A further difficulty arose when I attempted to compare *The Fellowship* with traditionally published books. This was based on the belief that publishers would probably shy away from this one because of the mix of genres. *The Fellowship* is both a crime thriller and a historical novel which makes it neither one nor the other for classification purposes. It has to be remembered that publishers' main interests are in selling the books they publish, and a mix of genres would create confusion for their marketing strategies.

There are those who consider crime novels cannot be literary novels. However *Agency Woman* by A A Logan disproves this. Once I started reading I found this book to be a literary feast. The writing was descriptive, with great imagery, and beautiful poetic prose. It was also a book capable of making a reader ponder the intricacies of the government's use of secret agencies. MI5 and MI6 spring to mind as well as America's CIA, and Russia's KGB.

The story is told in the first person, from the point of view of a retired agent who previously worked for the mysterious Scottish Agency, and from the first chapter I was sucked into the mystery that pervades the whole book. The burned-out retired agent, who at this stage is nameless, is abducted and subjected to torture from other employees of the Agency. He is sent on a mission with one of his captors, a beautiful, but ruthless woman.

The action takes place in a remote spot on the west coast of Scotland, and the mountain, which looms over the cottage they have rented, plays a large part in the story.

Mystery abounds in this book. Neither the reader nor the characters are aware of the nature of the mission, and move on to each part of the story after receiving orders from the Scottish Agency. The plotting is excellent with surprises aplenty, and with a surreal quality which helps to keep the reader guessing. Characterization is convincing, although we are never really sure of the motivation, or even the mental stability of each character, and it is some time before we know the real names of the amphibian, the cowboy, the big-headed man, and the red-shoed lady.

There is everything in this book – crime, murder, spies, terrorists, a sexual component, and of course the machinations of the Scottish Agency, with thrilling final scenes involving a helicopter chase, explosions and gunfire, leaving behind a multitude of bodies. Hanging over everything is the mystery of who and what the burned-out retired agent is capable of, and whether he will be able to resurrect his earlier life and experience within the Agency. And, of course, who will be left standing at the end of the novel.

This is a novel that qualifies on many grounds as a book that could easily have been marketed by one of the big publishers, although they might have experienced difficulty classifying it to fit a bookseller's shelves. Should it be placed as a literary novel, crime, thriller, adventure, or, as I have viewed it, a political crime thriller. suffice to say if a reader is looking for any of the above subgenres of crime, this book will fit very well.

Most readers have heard about hard-boiled fiction, but do we really know what it is? I was surprised to find that it was not as dark as I had expected, and many familiar scenarios are acted out in the hard-boiled world of crime fiction. My next chapter will examine this genre which has been around for quite a long time.

18

Hard-Boiled Crime Fiction

Hard-boiled crime fiction originated in America during the 1920s, and it rose to popularity at the same time as the more intellectual mystery and detective fiction of the golden age. The American hard-boiled crime, however, was vastly different from the puzzle stories Agatha Christie, and other golden age authors were publishing. In comparison to the intellectual sleuth of the mystery and detective genre, the hard-boiled sleuth was a gun for hire, a loner working on the edge of the law, fighting villains in a corrupt world of mean streets, relying on his fists and his own personal code of ethics.

The Oxford Companion to Crime & Mystery Writing when discussing hard-boiled fiction which was the domain of male authors writing about male private eyes, describes it thus *"The milieu was the underside of the city. Its mean streets reflected the cynicism of Prohibition, the disillusionment following World War 1, and later, the grimness of America during the Great Depression. His world was pervaded by greed, corruption, and alienation in the face of ill-defined but massive economic and social threats. Nonetheless, the private eye often maintained a personal, albeit bruised, faith in values he felt ought to be upheld in a fallen world."*

The early authors of the hard-boiled genre, such as Dashiell Hammett, and Raymond Chandler, introduced readers to the private eye; cynical, world weary detectives operating in a corrupt world. The style was terse and fast moving, and often interspersed with wisecracks, while violence was the norm in these action-packed thrillers. It was the age of the anti-hero, and other writers were soon to follow in what was to become a popular genre of crime fiction. Most of the stories the private eye inhabited were told from the first person point of view and the detective is speaking directly to his readers. He is usually a hard drinker who operates out of a shabby office, which normally contains a desk, a telephone, and a filing cabinet that is used to contain his whisky bottle. He frequents bars, eats in greasy spoon diners - you will rarely find him eating in a fancy restaurant - and he always carries a gun. Violence is part and parcel of his existence, and he will fight or shoot his way out of dangerous situations. Despite this, he has a code of conduct, and there are lines he will not cross.

Like most crime fiction, the hard-boiled genre has developed and changed over the years. There are still private eye novels, and crime is still committed on the 'mean streets', but I am not sure that Sam Spade or Mickey Spillane would still be conducting business in the modern world. They would have needed to move with the times. Hard-boiled fiction is now richer and deeper, the private eyes are no longer confined to macho male characters, although these characters are still tough. The violence and action is still there, as are the urban criminal environments.

The hard-boiled crime story has become the private eye story which many people think is an anomaly in today's world. But there are still detective agencies in the real world, and the literary private eye has adapted to modern times. He has become more rounded with up to date interests and life style, and may have a law enforcing back story. For example, he may be an ex-policeman. In all likelihood he will have a broken relationship in his past, possibly a divorce. He seldom has a wife, although he may have transitory love interests. The one thing the private eye has in common with his predecessors is his unique sense of justice.

Contemporary writers of private eye crime novels include: Robert Crais, with his Elvis Cole detective based in Hollywood; Reginald Hill, whose creation is the Luton based private eye, Joe Sixmith; and John Connolly, who brought Charlie 'Bird' Parker, an ex-NYPD detective, to the page. Their female counterparts include: Marcia Muller's part Shoshone Indian investigator, Sharon McCone; and Sara Paretsky's private eye, V.I. Warshawski of Chicago.

Stories with a private eye as the main character are still considered to be an American type of crime fiction, and certainly most authors of these novels are American. *The Oxford Companion to Crime & Mystery Writing* considers that attempts to launch private eye fiction in Britain have not been successful. This may be one of the reasons that John Connolly, who is Irish, sets his books in Maine, the home of Stephen King. However, I can think of at least two British authors who write in this genre - Reginald Hill, mentioned above, and Russell D. McLean, with his Dundee Private Investigator J. McNee. McLean, in particular, writes his prose in a hard-boiled style reminiscent of the American hard-boiled novels.

So far I have considered the differences between hard-boiled and traditional crime fiction, however, there are also similarities. There is a problem, a client consults the detective and seeks his help with a mystery to be solved, and the detective must solve the mystery. One aspect that is missing in the hard-boiled genre, is the intellectual summing up once the mystery has been solved, and the story reaches its conclusion in other ways.

The hard-boiled style originated in America and featured lone private investigators, so *Black* by Russell Blake seemed to fit the genre which was why I downloaded and read it. The main character, Artemis Black, fascinated me, with his hangups about his name, his parents, and his persona. His obsession with Humphrey Bogart (Bogey) affects his whole life. He dresses like him, drives an ancient Eldorado model Cadillac, and models himself on his hero in every way possible. This is offset by his wise-cracking goth receptionist, Roxie, who has tattoed arms, sings in an indie art rock band, and has a tough chick demeanour. He seems to be very much out of place in contemporary Los Angeles with his 1940s clothes, double-breasted jackets, and fedora hat.

His client, a washed-up Hollywood movie star is as unlikeable as his wife is glamorous. She was an admirable fit to the gorgeous dame of hard-boiled fiction, and Black spends a fair amount of time fighting off her advances. The plot was intricate with the paparazzi being bumped off at regular intervals, and Black's client in the frame as the killer. The plot was intricate with lots of action, including Black's beloved car being blown up. And it had a fantastic double twist at the end.

This book was well written with descriptive, dynamic writing as vivid as the lightning storm it started with. The dialogue was natural and in keeping with the hard-boiled style, particularly when he says, *"Screw everyone who thought he looked like a douche. He had style. Panache. Something that had passed into a byegone era."* He also goes on to say *"He could do a lot worse than to let a little Maltese Falcon slip into his life."* And for the uninitiated *The Maltese Falcon* was a Humphrey Bogart film which was adapted from a Dashiell Hammett book.

I enjoyed reading this book and felt it satisfied all the criteria for a hard-boiled detective novel. Black was a lone gun for hire, a Private Investigator (PI) who worked on the fringes of the law, always on the verge of insolvency, and he had his own code of ethics which he lived by. It would sit comfortably alongside any traditionally published novel in the same genre.

There were three reasons I chose *Hail Mary* by J R Rain. It had a good ranking on Amazon, the author has written a lot of books, and he is an ex-private investigator. At the very least he would have an inside knowledge of how a private investigator works.

Hail Mary introduces the reader to Jim Knighthorse, an ex-football player, now turned private investigator, with a footballer's physique, and a cocky manner. During the course of the book he is involved with three cases, which I am sure is more like real life than the usual crime investigation of only one case. The first of these cases involves the death of an activist by shark finners, although nothing is ever simple in the world of fiction. I learned a lot during this part of the book about how shark finners pursue their illegal occupation, and if you like dogs then you are going to be shocked by their use as shark bait. I was a bit disappointed that this case did not really have a resolution, although there was plenty of action, and the shark finners did get their comeuppance.

The case of the flasher in a gated community of retirees did get solved, although this case took up less time in the book. The third case was personal to Jim Knighthorse. It was his investigation into the twenty year old mystery of who murdered his mother. In my opinion the investigation of this case was the nearest this novel got to the hard-boiled genre. It involved action, a gun-toting private investigator, violence, and the solving of an old mystery.

The book was well written, although there were some proofing glitches. However, these were minimal and did not get in the way of reading enjoyment. It was written in the first person, and had a humorous wise-cracking style. the characterization was good and the plotting was adequate, although as previously indicated, I would have preferred more of a resolution to the shark finning episode. But I suppose this reflects the real life experience of a private investigator where not every case has a resolution.

In terms of hard-boiled crime fiction it did meet most of the criteria. The lone private investigator who is a gun for hire working on the fringes of the law, the wise-cracking style, and he did have his own moral code. However, the setting was more rural than urban, and the mean streets were lacking.

It can sometimes be risky to read a first novel because the writer may not yet have honed their writing skills. But I do like to read an author's first novel if I feel they measure up to a professional standard.

I need not have feared. Keith Dixon's first novel *Altered Life* was a good read with descriptive writing and good characterization, and I was pleased to see he was forensically aware.

Some of the descriptive passages I liked included *"a woman in her early forties with an over elaborate dress sense,"* the same woman had a *"swirl of dark hair that became lighter as it spiralled from her head, like cream dropped into coffee."* Another woman had *"hair the colour of sun-dried straw."* When describing the difference between places, he says, *"Waverley was Pashminas; Crewe was scarves."* There were many more passages I could have quoted, and they left me feeling that this was a writer who was adept at making the narrative come alive with his word pictures.

Again, this was a book that met the hard-boiled criteria with a lone PI (Private Investigator), working on the fringes of the law, and with his own code of ethics. Sam Dyke, the PI, was an ex-Customs and Excise officer, who only accepts a case if he thinks it fits in with his values. He turns down a case and the client is almost immediately murdered, leaving Sam with a guilt complex for not taking the client seriously.

The setting is Cheshire, and the book had everything needed

for a crime novel – murder, mystery, abduction, and action. There was conflict from the police who did not like Sam's meddling in the case, a bit of romantic suspense, and a surprising twist in chapter six that I did not see coming.

The only negative for me was the ending which seemed slightly out of character with the rest of the book. Sam Dyke is lured to a remote and dangerous place in a situation which is an obvious trap. I felt it would require a level of stupidity to follow through with such a meeting. Apart from that, the setting was more rural and completely different, and while there was action and suspense in this section it did test my suspension of disbelief.

However, the excellent plot, the descriptive writing, and the realistic characterization, more than made up for this shortcoming.

Hard-boiled fiction suggests male sleuths, but it does not necessarily have to be that way. Times are changing and women are infiltrating every area of crime fiction, both as writers and characters. So, in my next chapter I will be looking at women sleuths.

19

Female Sleuths

An early chapter of this book discusses the historical background of the crime novel and at the time of my research I did not notice that female sleuths were barely mentioned prior to the golden age of crime fiction. A reader could be forgiven for assuming that Agatha Christie's, Miss Marple, was a forerunner of the female investigator. But this is far from the truth.

There were many fictional female sleuths in the nineteenth century long before Miss Marple first appeared. Admittedly, many of these were published as dime novels in America. The dime novel, similar to a penny dreadful, was a generic name for American printed publications at this time. They were issued at regular intervals and some of the stories were quite lurid. Among the authors writing detective fiction featuring female sleuths for these publications were W Stephens Hayward, Harlan P Halsey writing as Old Sleuth, and Albert W Aitken. Of these authors Old Sleuth was the most prolific, although the others had many books to their credit. I was interested to note that in the section on dime novels in *The Oxford Companion to Crime and Mystery Writing* there is no mention of female detectives, although it gives a good overview of these publications. Few of the early female sleuths featured, or their authors, are to be found listed in any work concerning mystery or crime fiction, and it would appear they have slid into obscurity. This is possibly because of their origins in the dime novels of the 19th century, but it has to be remembered that this was where most detective novels were published at this time. It was also where more famous crime writers such as Dashiell Hammett and Raymond Chandler began their writing careers.

Research indicates that Andrew Forrester Jr was the first British writer to use a female sleuth in *The Female Detective* in 1864. However, there was an earlier author Catherine Crewe who wrote *The Adventures of Susan Hopley or Circumstantial Evidence* in 1841. Catherine L Pirkis, another British author, introduced the reader to her female sleuth Loveday Brooke in *The Experiences of Loveday Brooke, Lady Detective* in 1894. Then in 1897, Anna Katharine Green, an American author, published *The Affair Next Door* featuring Amelia Butterworth. She followed this up with a second female sleuth, Violet Strange, in 1915. It has been said that Agatha Christie was influenced by Green's Amelia Butterworth when she introduced Miss Marple. What is certain is that Agatha Christie was aware of Anna Katharine Green's writing and her use of female sleuths.

More recent additions to crime fiction featuring female sleuths include Patricia Cornwell's Kay Scarpetta, Lynda La Plante's DCI Jane Tennison in the *Prime Suspect* series, Sara Paretsky's V.I. Warshawski, Val McDermid's Carol Jordan, and Thomas Harris's Clarice Starling.

Female sleuths would therefore appear to be more prolific than is apparent when reading about the history of crime fiction. In Barry Forshaw's *The Rough Guide to Crime Fiction*, he states, *"One of the most interesting developments of the form – and a relatively recent one at that – is the introduction of female private investigators (notably Sue Grafton's Kinsey Millhone and Sara Paretsky's V.I. Warshawski)."* It is his statement that the female sleuth is a recent development that I find interesting, considering there were many predecessors dating back to the 19th century.

The first book I read for the female sleuths section was published by a small independent publisher *Kozy Kat Press*. It was *Truth Kills (An Angelina Bonaparte Mystery)*, by Nanci Rathbun. This was an excellent read with an intriguing main character Angelina Bonaparte or Angie for short.

The book is an American private investigator mystery, and is set in Milwaukee in south-east Wisconsin on the shores of Lake Michigan.

I particularly liked the main character in this book Angelina Bonaparte who is aged 50, and is an American private investigator with a Sicilian family background. She is a divorcee with an adult family who now have families of their own. She has her own apartment, leads a single lifestyle, drives a Black Cherry Miata car, and has the occasional sexual encounter. Her father is old-style Italian/Sicilian with Mafia connections, and he disapproves of her choice of career and how she lives her life.

Here is how Angelina describes herself – *"I'm a professional snoop and I'm good at it. While on the job, I can look like the senior partner of an accountancy firm in my pinstripe suit, or the neighbourhood white-haired old-lady gossip. Off the job, I'm a fifty-something hottie: white hair gelled back, dramatic eye make-up, toned body encased in designer duds. Gravity has taken a small toll, but who notices in candlelight?"* When the reader first meets her, she is dressed as a bag lady because she intends to investigate a rubbish skip. However, it is obvious that in her leisure time she dresses smartly, is attractive, and has a modern appearance and lifestyle.

Angelina is employed by a solicitor to prove the innocence of his client, Tony Belloni, following the murder of Tony's mistress. Angelina is convinced that Tony is not the murderer, and she is determined to prove his innocence. In the process the story becomes an excellent mystery in terms of whodunit. It kept me guessing right until the end.

I liked the wisecracking hard-boiled style of the writing. It was fast-paced, and there was a hint of romance in the story. The plotting was excellent, and there were no problems with the editing.

This book is engaging, interesting, and kept me guessing. All the ingredients for a good murder mystery. This book is equal to any traditionally published book on the bookstore shelves.

My next choice, *Hushabye* by Celina Grace, was a really good read. The female sleuth was Detective Sergeant Kate Redman, a complex character with private issues of her own to deal with as well as solving the murder mystery.

This novel was a British police procedural with all the elements that make a good crime story. A ruthless millionaire, a trophy wife, a murder, the abduction of a baby, plus plenty of skulduggery happening along the way. It all contributed to a fast-paced exciting story.

There was no gore or violence in this novel, so it could equally have fitted the cosy category as well as female sleuth, and police procedural. The structure, plot, and characterization were all excellent, and I would definitely place this writer on my list of authors to follow. There were a very small number of proofing errors, but apart from that the structural editing was impeccable. And these minor proofing issues did not interfere with my enjoyment of the book.

J.A. Konrath is a legend in the indie self-publishing community. Initially a traditionally published author, he converted to self-publishing and is one of its biggest champions. He sells thousands of indie books and his blog *A Newbie's Guide to Publishing* is followed by millions.

When I started to read *Bloody Mary*, by J.A. Konrath, the second book in his Jack Daniels series, it soon became obvious why he is so popular and has many followers.

Jacqueline Daniels, known to her colleagues as Jack Daniels, is a forty something cop in Chicago. She is partnered by the slovenly, overweight Herb Benedict. Both are dedicated detectives and set off on the trail of a serial killer who is littering the city with body parts.

Jack also has personal issues. An elderly mother at risk living on her own but who still has the energy to indulge in sexual antics with an equally ancient boyfriend; an ex-husband who wants to return to the fold; a devoted new boyfriend who wants her to commit; and to top it all a psycho cat.

This book is well written and plotted, with unexpected twists. It flows well, with excellent characterization and dialogue interspersed with laugh-out-loud humour as well as black humour. The pace and suspense make this a page-turner, and the action-packed ending ratchets up the tension to an almost unbearable level. This novel straddles the subgenres. It is a competent police procedural, it fits the female sleuth subgenre, the mystery and detective category, and the humour section. In fact, it could probably fit any of the subgenres discussed in this book.

In my opinion *Bloody Mary* would slot easily into a traditional publisher's list, but I doubt very much that J.A. Konrath would be interested.

Moving on now to a subgenre that is becoming ever more popular – the police procedural.

20

The Police Procedural

Detective and crime fiction often have police characters. In many earlier crime novels, these have been secondary characters and are often depicted as being less intelligent than the amateur detective. The two most obvious policemen to fall into this category are – Arthur Conan Doyle's bumbling Inspector Lestrade, and Agatha Christie's dogged Inspector Japp. Then, as crime fiction developed, the police character as the main investigator, became more common. But many of these were stories about one central police character, such as Simenon's Inspector Jules Maigret, or Ngaio Marsh's Chief Inspector, later Superintendent, Roderick Alleyn. But these are not police procedurals.

This begs the question as to what a police procedural is. It is not just the use of a main police character. *The Oxford Companion to Crime & Mystery Writing* states that *"By contrast, the police procedural features a collective, such as a homicide squad, as leading protagonists. Their detection methods derive from their real-life counterparts in organized police forces: routine interrogation, lots of legwork, digging into bureaucratic records, forensic technology, the use of informants, and trial and error."*

In America, Lawrence Treat's 1945 novel *V as in Victim* is often cited as being the first true police procedural. While, in Britain, it is thought to be Morris Proctor's *The Chief Inspector's Statement*, also known as *The Pennycross Murders*, published in1951. In Britain, John Creasey (writing as J.J.

Marric), wrote more than twenty books in the 1950s, featuring Scotland Yard detective, George Gideon, starting with *Gideon's Way*. While, in the US, Ed McBain was writing the *87th Precinct* series. More recent writers include John Harvey with his Detective Inspector Charlie Resnick, or Reginald Hill's series featuring Dalziel and Pascoe, Ruth Rendell's Detective Chief Inspector Reginald Wexford, and many others.

One disadvantage of police procedurals, is that the procedure is the primary focus in the investigation, and that can often be at the expense of character development, although many authors manage to combine characterization with plot. My own preference is for a police procedural that also has psychological elements, as well as characters with whom I can empathize. My own crime novels are not pure police procedurals, although they are often described as such, because my police characters are secondary characters, although the procedural aspects are correct.

So, in looking for police procedurals for my reading list, I decided my criteria should include, police characters as the main protagonists, they should be investigating a crime or crimes, follow procedure, and if possible bring in forensics, as well as a taste of the bureaucracy modern police forces have to take in their stride.

The first of my three choices of police procedurals was *Ghost in the Machine*, by Ed James, who is an Edinburgh author, so I thought it would be a good choice for the Edinburgh e-Book Festival. Apart from that, the majority of the reviews on Amazon were four and five stars with a smattering of three and one solitary two star review. So, what did I think of it?

To start with, it was an easy, if somewhat simplistic, read. It followed a single plotline, and within that framework it met all the requirements for a police procedural. The characters did lack depth, but this can be a common failing of police procedurals because the main focus is on the investigation, the police team, and the procedures. This was a dialogue driven book, and the only descriptive parts concerned Edinburgh and its environs, which were on the whole, accurate. I did wonder at the start whether this was a book I was going to enjoy, and the overuse of speech tags in some parts, irritated me a bit. But I am a stickler when it comes to things like that, and someone with less of a proofreading eye will probably not notice.

Other things I found less than credible were issues to do with the command structure of the police in this book. The main police character, Scott Cullen, was a detective constable, which made an agreeable change from the usual inspectors etc. But this was where my suspension of disbelief was tested because Scott acted more like a senior officer. He gave orders to others of the same rank, he argued with his superiors, on one occasion he even rapped a senior's fingers over the actions he had taken. Somehow or other, I do not think a senior officer would have found that acceptable, nor do I think his colleagues would have found his actions endearing.

However, as I read on I got drawn into the story. The plot was good, the investigation was good, and it had an exciting end. What more could a reader want?

The second book I chose for this section, *The Scars Beneath the Soul,* by Dave Sivers, was a well written police procedural. It was competent, well plotted, and the characters appealed to me.

Lizzie Archer moves from the Metropolitan Police to become a detective inspector with the Aylesbury Vale Division of Thames Valley Police. This is initially resented by Dan Baines who has to return to being a detective sergeant despite filling the inspector's post on a temporary basis. The problems between them are exacerbated when Lizzie Archer thinks that Baines pays too much attention to her scarred face, a disfigurement obtained in the line of duty. However, they have to work together as a team, and they form an uneasy relationship.

Archer is immediately plunged into a vicious murder, which is closely followed by other murders. The investigation is not helped by the frequent sightings by Baines of his missing son, who may or may not be dead. Nor is it helped by an obstructive senior officer, and a negligent colleague. Lines of enquiry are followed, and the frustration of the investigating officers is palpable. Meanwhile, a child runs away after accidentally shooting his brother with the gun he found on the estate where he lives.

What I liked most about this book was the realistic portrayal of the everyday life of police investigating teams, and the balancing act necessary to cope with conflicting demands. The frictions which beset working relationship and how these are resolved. There was also a definite feel of how individual officers balanced their personal lives and their likes and dislikes, while getting on with the job.

Archer and Baines become increasingly harassed as they deal with the rising body count, a serial murder, and a gun-toting child on the run. And the pace continues to rise until the action-packed ending.

This is a book that should satisfy any reader who enjoys police procedurals, and it is a match for many traditionally published in this genre.

My next choice was *Steps to Heaven*, by Wendy Cartmell. This was a police procedural with a difference because the main character was an army investigator, and the setting was Aldershot Garrison.

This story was well plotted with believable characters, and it kept the element of mystery to the forefront. I was so drawn into the story that I didn't even register until I was quite some distance through the book that the author was the narrator, and she was telling the story, rather than the characters showing the reader what was happening. I am not a lover of the omniscient point of view because I think it puts a space between the story and the reader, so it is a tribute to the author that she was writing in this style, but it wasn't immediately obvious.

The ending was action packed and exciting, although I couldn't help thinking that with a different point of view – perhaps the main character's – the element of suspense could have been ratcheted to a higher level. However, this was a well written, absorbing book with enough mystery and action to satisfy most readers of crime fiction.

My next two choices were less enjoyable, and I stopped reading both of them when I was about thirty per cent into the story. The first one was spot on with the procedural element, but the storyline was less obvious. Maybe if I'd stuck with it, the story would have developed; however, it was mainly narrative with bits of unconvincing dialogue thrown in now and again. It was also written in a rather factual way which would have been more suited to a report than a fictional story, and the punctuation was all over the place, particularly in the dialogue sections.

The second one suffered from loads of information dumps. Each time a character was introduced the writer gave his or her biography, most of which was unnecessary to the development of the story. This book had a political theme, but by the time I had reached thirty percent, the political aspects were still being explained with only a couple of short bits reflecting the police procedures, although the procedures were again spot on.

I chose both of these books because they were written by policemen, which was probably why the procedural parts of the story were so accurate, but I am afraid these bits overshadowed the story so much that the storyline was not obvious. When I think about it, the reason I never make any of my main characters a social worker is because having worked in the profession I am far too close to it and I suspect that I would also have fallen into the trap of report-like writing if I did have a social worker protagonist. Sometimes when you are too familiar with a particular job or profession it can work against your imagination, and I suspect this is what happened with both these books.

The next book I chose was *The Darkness*, by Bill Kirton. Many police procedurals deal with more than one crime throughout the story, similar to what real life cops do, and this book was no exception. The story followed two different crimes, one was a whodunit, and the other was a whydunit. So this book was more than a police procedural, it was also a dark crime story with a strong psychological element. The story described the police procedural parts realistically, and the sense of bureaucracy and frustration that affects the daily life of cops was well handled. However, the psychological element where the reader is taken inside the mind of a man who started out with abductions and turned into a killer, was brilliant. I could almost imagine being tied to a pillar in the cellar of the perpetrator's house. Meanwhile, the whodunit had a twist, and the killer was not the obvious suspect. I'll say no more, you'll have to read the book to find out.

So in this post I read four whole books and part of two additional ones, and in my opinion the best came last.

Dark and noir crime fiction are now very popular, and many readers assume this is a recent addition to crime fiction, but they would be wrong. Noir crime novels have been around for some considerable time, and in my next chapter I will be examining the dark side of crime fiction.

21

Noir/Dark Crime Fiction

I have always been a lover of crime fiction, starting with Agatha Christie's cosy crime puzzles, graduating to authors like P.D. James and Ruth Rendell, and moving on to Val McDermid and Mo Hayder. Now I am sure many lovers of crime fiction will notice that as my reading progressed it gradually became darker and darker. This made me reflect on how crime fiction has developed over the years.

When I first started reading crime fiction, the puzzle was the most important thing. The book would start with a death, clues would be given. It was then a race between author and reader as to which of them solved the crime first, and the characters were chess pieces, to be moved about on a board. I continued to read in this fashion for many years. However, I think it was after reading the first Patricia Cornwell book *Post Mortem,* I realized that characters were also pivotal in crime fiction, and they could have their own stories which were not necessarily part of the crime.

The crime novel had become character driven, and of course this made risk and danger more immediate, and the stories darker. But there are degrees of darkness, right up to the modern noir novel.

Searching for a definition of noir crime fiction on the internet comes up with a variety of definitions, and each new source seems to have a different one. The Meriam-Webster Dictionary definition states: *"Taken from the French word meaning 'darkness' or 'of the night,' noir is a category of modern crime fiction. Used for fiction of crime and detection, often in a grim urban setting, featuring petty, amoral criminals and other down-and-out characters, and permeated by a feeling of disillusionment, pessimism and despair."*

On the other hand, the American noir genre, rose from the hard-boiled detective fiction written in the 1920s and 30s by writers such as Dashiel Hammett, and Raymond Chandler. Peter Haining writing in Barry Forshaw's *British Crime Writing: An Encyclopedia; Vol 2*, says that *"British noir was the illegitimate offspring of American hard-boiled fiction,"* and that it was *"fostered through the ominous days before and after the Second World War."* He describes it as having *"solitary heroes, femme fatales, crime and murder,"* and that it *"captured the anxieties, preoccupations and grim moral code of the times in which they were written."*

However, although noir is said to be a subset of the hard-boiled style, there are differences because the protagonist is not usually a detective. The main character is often a victim, a suspect or a perpetrator and is tied directly to the crime, rather like my own main characters. And the story often includes sex and violence with common themes being depravity, and amorality. A far cry from Agatha Christie type stories.

The first British noir novels are credited to William Roland Daniel, an American born writer who lived in Britain. He published *The Gangster* in 1932, followed by *The Gangster's Last Shot* in 1939, and during his lifetime he produced over 200 books.

Underworld characters and crime are often the mark of a noir novel, and Hugh Desmond Clevely first introduced this theme in *The Crime Smasher* in 1937. Other early writers of noir fiction include Richard Goyne, William J Elliott, Peter Cheyney, James Hadley Chase, and Hank Janson. The best known contemporary author of noir fiction is, of course, James

Ellroy.

However, with the increasing darkness of many crime novels it is becoming difficult to separate dark fiction from the truly noir novel. So, given the many definitions of noir novels, I decided to concentrate on dark crime novels, many of which could also be described as noir.

My first choice in the area of dark crime was *The Rotting Spot,* by Valerie Laws. The title intrigued me, and it had many excellent reviews, so I reckoned it must be a reasonably good read, and it didn't disappoint me. The plot was compelling, it kept me guessing – I like to be kept guessing, but it is becoming increasingly difficult – and the characters were original and engaging. The main character, Erica Bruce, is a homeopath, an exercise and keep fit freak, a borderline anorexic who fights to retain a balance between eating, fitness and health. She jogs and, wait for it, collects the skulls of dead animals as a hobby! Now how much more original than that can you be?

The darkness in this story comes from the many dysfunctional characters the reader meets along the way. One of them speaks with a distinctive Geordie accent, and although I often have problems reading books that use accents in dialogue, I had no problems following this one. The story revolves round a girl who has been missing for 25 years, her dysfunctional family, and her cousin who goes missing during the course of the story.

In many ways, this story met the criteria of a cosy, although a lot darker. It had the amateur sleuth, the unbelieving detective, and a great mystery. I don't think it met the criteria of noir, not hard-boiled enough, but it certainly met the criteria of dark. If there were such a subgenre, I would be tempted to call it a dark cosy. One more thing, the language and descriptions were so vivid, I could see them, and when I looked at the author's background I wasn't surprised to find out she is also a poet. I'll be looking out for more books by this author.

My next choice was *Kicking Off,* by Jan Needle, and I was breathless by the time I reached the end. This was a very dark, gritty novel with various characters rather than a main protagonist; however, it was easy to follow the stories of each individual character. The main thrust of the novel was prison riots, starting off with a riot at Buckie Prison, leading up to a major riot at Bowscar Prison. There was political intrigue and corruption along the way, and I do like political shenanigans in a novel. The violence was extreme, as was the sex, but it was a roller coaster of a read and illustrated what could happen when a prison reaches boiling point. There were some seriously unlikable characters among the prisoners, but their violence and aggression was out in the open, not like the politicians attempting to sweep everything under the carpet and in the process becoming the real villains of the piece.

This was a book filled with raw emotion, double dealing, brutalized men, murder, and rape. The suspense and tension mounts chapter by chapter until it reaches an explosive end. I reckon this book could easily fit into the noir genre, and I'll be looking out for more books by Jan Needle.

Next came *Hamelin's Child,* by Debbie Bennett. This dark novel of child abduction and rent boys is the story of Michael, an ordinary middle-class boy, who is drugged and abducted on his seventeenth birthday. Three weeks later he wakes up as Mikey, a heroin addict who is required to service male clients. At first he fights against his new life but soon gives in to pressure from his abductors in order to maintain his heroin supply.

This book can be shocking in parts, but at no time is compassion for Mikey lost, even after he accepts his situation, develops an attachment to his captors, and no longer wants to go home. The author is expert at handling Mikey's conflicting emotions, as well as describing his dependence on his captors and the heroin they supply to him. The reader is desperate for Mikey to find his way back to being Michael, but is left with the feeling that there is no way out for him, and that even if he does find his way home it would be unrealistic to expect everything to be the same.

This book is a well-written, hard-hitting novel of a life that will be unfamiliar to most readers, and there is no doubt in my mind that it was a perfect fit for the noir genre.

Phew! These novels have left me breathless, but that's the way I like my reading to affect me, and I hope you've enjoyed your journey to the dark side. Now, why don't you move on to the next chapter where I'll be discussing Tartan Noir.

22

Tartan Noir/Scottish Crime

You have probably come across references to Tartan Noir on the internet and various other places, and if you walk into a bookstore in Scotland, the chances are you will see a display labelled Tartan Noir. But what is Tartan Noir?

The name is an odd mix. The tartan part of the name smacks of tourism, kilts, heather and bagpipes, all the stuff that attracts people to Scotland, although it is not all that relevant in today's modern world. The second part of the title – Noir – is more reminiscent of blood and gore, and all the horrible things that happen in the darkest of crime fiction. So it is an odd mix indeed.

It was actually James Ellroy who coined the name when he referred to Ian Rankin as the King of Tartan Noir in the 1990s. Since then it seems to have been taken up to describe Scottish crime fiction in general, and has now been given historical antecedents.

The origins of Tartan Noir in Scottish literature are claimed to be rooted in the works of James Hogg, Robert Louis Stevenson and William McIlvaney.

James Hogg's *Confessions of a Justified Sinner,* written in 1824, seems to be the earliest influence. This novel has been variously described as a psychological case study; a gothic novel with elements of horror; a satire of extreme theology; plus an early example of crime fiction. The book is said to be the earliest example of a novel using an alter-ego, and involves a battle between good and evil. Hogg's novel was also reputed to have an influence on *Jekyll and Hyde*, by Robert Louis Stevenson, as well as James Robertson's novel, *The Testament of Gideon Mack*.

Jekyll and Hyde, written by Stevenson in 1886 uses split personality, and continues the theme of the battle between good and evil. He claims the idea came to him in a nightmare and he called it *"a fine bogy tale."* In her essay *The Dark Threads of Tartan Noir*, Carole E. Barrowman writes – *"Like every noir writer since then, Stevenson situates evil in the heart of man, and then places that man in the heart of a city. The city becomes a manifestation of the moral hypocrisy and the mock respectability that the noir writer attacks."*

Tartan Noir was also heavily influenced by American writers such as Dashiell Hammett, Raymond Chandler, and James Ellroy, who were all writing hard-boiled detective fiction. Many Scottish authors followed in their footsteps, probably beginning with William McIlvaney, who has been termed the Godfather of Tartan Noir, a title that bemuses him. When he wrote *Laidlaw*, he said he had no intention of writing a crime novel. He wanted to write a story that was real, not one where the book was taken up with a murder and whodunit. It just happened that the character he chose was a detective with a troubled past and present.

Many Scots have a fascination for gruesome events, particularly those that have happened in the past, therefore it is not surprising that Burke and Hare, the body snatchers who operated in Edinburgh between 1827-1828, and Deacon Brodie, a respectable town councillor by day and a housebreaker at night, are considered influential in the rise of the type of dark writing labelled noir. In fact, Deacon Brodie is considered to be another of the influences behind the writing of Stevenson's *Jekyll and Hyde*.

So where does that take us in defining Tartan Noir? Is it the broad sweep of Scottish crime fiction, or is it a subset of hard-boiled and dark crime, that takes the reader to a dark and scary place?

Maybe if we look at the issues Tartan Noir novels explore, that will help us decide. These include psychological and socio-economic issues, hard-boiled crime, and dark crime. The people in these books are invariably flawed, often with split personalities, and the main characters are anti-heroes rather than heroes. So does this rule out cosy crime? And how dark does dark crime have to be? Or is it safer to include all Scottish crime? I don't know.

However, it seems to me that if a crime novel is written by a Scottish author and is set in Scotland, then it will be included in the Tartan Noir section of a lot of bookshops, so maybe we are just looking at Scottish crime fiction, which has been given a fancy name.

So with all this buzzing round my mind I went on a trawl of the internet to find crime novels to fit in with this criteria.

The first author I discovered was Sinclair MacLeod, and I downloaded his novel, *The Reluctant Detective*. It was set in Glasgow, and the main character was an insurance investigator who became involved in a murder investigation which had been written off by the police as a suicide.

This book met the criteria of Scottish crime fiction, although I would hesitate to call it Tartan Noir because it wasn't particularly dark. The story followed the format of a traditional mystery and was probably closer to a cosy crime novel than a noir one. However, I did find it an enjoyable read, and an entertaining mystery, although I found the disclosure of the crime by the perpetrator at the end of the book to be more in the style of an Agatha Christie explanation of what had happened than a modern interpretation of the crime.

The next book I read was *Saturday Night and Sunday*

Morning, a novella by Mark Frankland. This was another book I enjoyed reading, although I found the narrative style a bit unusual, perhaps veering more to the literary than an action packed read. It tells the story of three teenagers who go out on the same Saturday night and how the events they encounter changes their lives forever. This was not a mystery story or a tale of murder, simply the telling of the lives of a junkie, a wheelchair bound man disabled by the violence he met that night, and an alcoholic single mother. Their lives are unpleasant and hopeless, and they are unable to get out of the downward spiral that is destroying them. I would certainly class this as a noir story, dealing with gritty social issues. So, yes, it is Tartan Noir.

Another new author for me was Peter Carroll, and I read his first published novel, *In Many Ways*. This was a hard hitting book set in Glasgow, and written by a Scot, so it was unquestionably Scottish crime fiction. The story deals with the underbelly of Glasgow, the gangsters, drug lords and junkies, and the ineffectiveness of the police in dealing with the problems they generate. The book is tough, violent and gritty, and amply meets the Tartan Noir label.

However, I did have a problem with the structure of the story, because as each character was introduced there was a lengthy description of their lives, which slowed the story down to a crawl, and I felt these parts were overwritten. No doubt the back stories of the characters were interesting, and many readers may like this, but I did feel the pace suffered. In contrast, the pace during the action sequences where the plot was moving forward, was so fast it left me breathless.

On balance, I did like this book. It was well written, and I thought the plot was good while the pace in the action scenes made it a page turner, although the same could not be said for the back story and descriptive scenes.

I do have some regrets that I didn't choose one of Peter Carroll's subsequent books rather than the first one because the excerpt I read for his second novel *Pandora's Pitbull* was full of pace and action packed, which is the way I like my crime fiction.

I enjoyed the next book I selected, *No Stranger to Death* by Janet O'Kane, although it wasn't what I expected. I had anticipated a traditional crime story with a Scottish setting. One that would fit into my Tartan Noir section. However, although there was murder and mystery in the novel, it was more of a character led story than a tightly plotted murder, mystery. That does not mean there was no plot, because there was. But the plot centred round the characters and what happened when murder made its entrance into their tight-knit community. This resulted in the murder becoming a plot device rather than the central, overarching theme of the book.

The main character, Zoe, becomes involved in the murder mystery part by discovering a murder victim in a Guy Fawkes bonfire. Events spiral from there, but the main focus is on Zoe and her life, both past and present, and I was more interested in the mysteries of Zoe's past than I was in who committed the first murder. There is a hint of an investigation, but this comes over more as curiosity on the part of the main characters, and the police are peripheral to the action. There is also action, and Zoe's life is under threat early in the book as well as later on in a thrilling finish.

The book was well written, well plotted, and totally believable. The dialogue was natural, and the characterization was excellent. I really cared about Zoe and her friend Kate, and I was afraid for them.

A most enjoyable book which bookstores might be happy to place on their shelves in either the crime category or the more general fiction category.

Now that I have worked my way through the darker categories of crime fiction it is time to look at serial killers, and why we find them so fascinating!

23

Serial Killers in Crime Fiction

Murder is not a new thing, and many novels have taken that as their theme, generating a fully fledged crime fiction genre. So, it is not surprising that crime writers have based stories around serial murder and serial killers. With that in the forefront of my mind I decided to look at serial killers in crime fiction. But to begin with, I thought I would give some thought to serial murder and serial killers. What, exactly, makes one killer a serial killer and another one not?

According to the Free Online Dictionary a serial killer is *"A person who murders three or more people over a period of more than thirty days, with a 'cooling off' period between each murder, and whose motivation for killing is largely based on psychological gratification."*

The FBI's definition is *"someone who murders at least three people with significant pauses between incidents. A mass murderer is defined as someone who kills at least four people simultaneously or within a short period of time. Spree killers are also classified separately from serial killers by the FBI, these murderers kill in different locations but within a short time frame. Serial killers work alone and kill strangers."*

These are rather simplistic definitions of what a serial killer is, but for the purposes of this book, it is sufficient. If you want to explore the phenomenon of serial murder and serial killers, a simple Google search will give you sufficient material to keep you reading for several days.

The concept of serial murder is attributed to Robert Ressler in the 1970s, although there is some debate that the terminology may have been used at an earlier date. The term was coined to refer to stranger murders, which was what they were known as prior to this. However, serial killers did not emerge following the application of this term, they have always been with us. You have to look no further than Jack the Ripper, in Victorian London.

Most killers slide into obscurity after a time, but the serial killer remains in the public consciousness, and in many cases they become even more notorious as time passes. Books are written about them, films and TV series are made, so it is not surprising that serial murder has become a theme for crime fiction. And, because of the fascination many people have with this type of crime, the books are invariably successful.

Many well known writers such as Patricia Cornwell, Jeffrey Deaver, Michael Connolly, and Val McDermid, to name just a few have presented their readers with serial killers. And there are few crime readers who are not familiar with Hannibal Lecter. But the books I wanted to look at were the lesser known names in the e-book world.

The first book I read was a novella by Scott Nicholson, *Crime Beat*. This was an American crime book, and I have many American authors among my favourites. I like the easy writing style that many of them have, almost conversational, and this novella did not disappoint. It was a fast read and a page turner. Set in the newspaper world the main character was the editor. But this was not the hectic, rat race type of media setting, it was a newspaper in a sleepy Appalachian town which suddenly has a crime wave after a new crime beat reporter joins the paper. The crime wave escalates to include serial murders and is a fascinating read. I loved the twist at the end, although I started to have an inclination it was coming, but then, I read a lot of crime fiction! This is definitely an author I will read again.

The next book I read I gave up on when only thirty per cent in. By that time, I'd got to the point where I couldn't stand the misspellings, grammatical errors, and flaky punctuation. The punctuation in particular meant I often had to read a passage twice in order to ascertain the meaning intended. It was a shame really because it had the makings of a good story.

So, because this book had to be scrapped from my list, I went back to do another internet trawl for a serial killer book to take its place. And I am really glad I did because the book I downloaded was fantastic. Brilliant plot, original characters, and a real page turner. The book was *Angel Killer*, written by Andrew Mayne.

The main character in *Angel Killer* is FBI agent, Jessica Blackwood, a magician before she joined the FBI. She becomes involved in the investigation of a series of murders, which everyone thinks are impossible and have a supernatural element. So, not only is there the mystery about the identity of the serial killer, nicknamed the Warlock, there is also the mystery of how he staged his crimes. This book was a rattling good read, although I felt I would have liked a little bit more about the Warlock at the end. The main character was excellent, the crimes were devious and well thought out, the investigation was enthralling, and there was a thrilling episode at the end of the book involving Jessica. However, the Warlock himself was a bit of an anticlimax.

My third choice was *The Easy Inside*, by Tom Goddard. This was a first book by a new author, so I wasn't sure what to expect. Many authors do not get into their stride until the second or third book, but there were no worries on that score with this book. It was so well written I had to keep checking that it actually was a first book. It was brilliant. The plot was good, the characters believable, and the setting unusual.

This book was set in a women's prison, a closed community where a serial killer known as the Hairdresser is killing off the inmates and then scalping them. Alongside this runs another investigation, because in order to get the co-operation of one of the inmates, the policeman involved in the case agrees to reinvestigate her case and prove her innocence. So not only is this story about serial killing inside a women's prison, it also involves a more traditional investigation outside the prison, and the mix works well.

I enjoyed the mystery element in this book, the fast pace and the suspense, and it kept me guessing. As soon as the author writes another book, I will be first in line to buy it.

I have spent a lot of time in this book talking about and studying indie crime novels. But what I haven't done, so far, is look at the indie novels which have been picked up by traditional publishers, and the indie authors forsaking independence for a publishing deal. I will rectify this in the next chapter.

24
Traditional Authors with Indie Roots

Independent publishing by the new breed of indie authors is growing at a phenomenal rate. Some of these writers, often referred to as hybrid authors, have previously been published traditionally, and some have a foot in both camps by publishing some of their books independently and others for a mainstream publishing house. Then there is the indie author who has never published any other way. Some of them may have tried the traditional route, only for their books to be swallowed up by the infamous slush pile, while others have circumvented that by diving straight into indie publishing. Among these writers will be many who strive to attract the attention of the big publishers through their success in the indie market, but there will also be others who no longer see a traditional publishing contract as something to aim for.

The slush pile is something that is known and hated by authors worldwide. It conjures up a vision of mountains of manuscripts vanishing under the weight of other, newer submissions, and indeed this was the case in many publishing houses, although I doubt if these slush piles still exist in their original form. The rumour has it that publishers are now using indie published e-books as the new slush pile, and many indie authors live for the day when their book will be recognized as literary gold and a publisher will appear waving a cheque for a massive amount of money. However, for most of them, this will never happen.

Publishing is a business, and businesses operate to make a

profit, therefore the one sure way to attract a publisher's attention is by proving your book can make money. Quality may come into it to a certain extent, but it is not an essential. The uptake of *Fifty Shades of Grey* is proof of that. I understand that the amount of downloads that will attract the attention of publishers, is anything in excess of 250,000. Now, a writer may achieve that by writing an outstanding book that takes the reading world by storm. On the other hand, there are writers who are very savvy at marketing, and this is the way they increase their sales figures. And, of course, the writer who can combine both of these skills deserves any success they achieve.

One of the problems working against an indie writer attracting the attention of a mainstream publisher is that indie e-books often get a bad press because of the amount of badly written, badly edited, and badly formatted e-books available on the internet, Amazon included. This has arisen because the e-book market is a free one, available to everyone who thinks they are undiscovered novelists. So, there is a mix of excellent e-books, good e-books, and dire ones. This has had the effect of making many readers look at all indie books with suspicion. But, as I have argued all the way through this book, there are indie books on sale which are as good as, and sometimes better than those published the traditional way.

Many mainstream authors condemn the indie published book out of hand, and often quote that writers with a well written book should be able to get a publishing contract. It is possible they are living in the past when this may have been the case, however, it is not so easy, in today's economic climate, to get that elusive publishing deal.

Writers often pursue the indie path to publishing when all else has failed. No doubt that will include a percentage of writers whose books are not of a sufficiently high standard to merit publication. But it also includes writers whose work is so good it is less easy to understand why a publishing deal eludes them.

The argument about publishers acting as gatekeepers and publishing books which are well written while rejecting those of a lesser quality, does not, in any case, hold water. Otherwise how explainable is it that John Kennedy Toole's great American novel *A Confederency of Dunces* was rejected by publishers over and over again, and yet it went on to win the Pulitzer Prize for fiction, twelve years after the author's death.

Likewise, if the publishers' gatekeeping was successful, there would be no need to offer contracts to indie writers who have achieved a measure of success. But several indie authors have been welcomed into the traditional fold. Authors such as Amanda Hocking who accepted a two million dollar contract from St Martins Press after self-publishing seventeen young-adult, supernatural suspense novels. Then there was John Locke who signed a limited deal with Simon & Schuster after selling over two million copies of his indie books. Joe Konrath and Barry Eisler signed with Amazon Encore for some of their books, so they fit the profile of hybrid authors who publish both ways. And, of course, the recent sensational success of *Fifty Shades of Grey*, written by E.L. James, was self-published before being acquired by Vintage. More recently there has been Mark Edwards and Louise Voss, Paul Pilkington, James Oswald, and Kerry Wilkinson.

Other indie authors have been approached by traditional publishers, but have decided not to accept the publishing offers made, preferring to retain their independence as writers and publishers. For example, Brenna Aubrey's contemporary romance novel was subject to a bidding war with four publishers, but she turned down a six-figure, three-book publishing contract, because she did not like the contract terms and preferred to stay an indie. Then there was Barry Eisler, who in 2011, turned down a publishing deal rumoured to be in the region of half a million dollars. Joe Konrath has also refused to sign with publishers, although I believe he is currently a hybrid author. A search of the internet will highlight other writers who prefer to remain as indie authors, rather than lose their independence to the demands of a publishing contract.

However, it is not only indie authors who are reinventing themselves as traditionally published authors. The opposite is also happening where authors are leaving their publishers to become indies. Lawrence Block, a well known American crime writer who has won many awards, including the prestigious Edgar and Shamus Awards, has embraced indie publishing. Traditionally he has published well over 100 books, some of which have been made into films. Then there is Dean Wesley Smith who also published over 100 novels over a thirty year period. His books include the only two original *Men in Black* novels, a couple of dozen *Star Trek* novels, *Spider-Man* and *X-Men* novels, as well as many more.

With the exception of the traditionally published authors who have never considered doing anything else, it appears there are now several avenues for authors to publish their books. There are the authors who only publish independently, the indies. The authors who have turned their backs on traditional publishing and have reinvented themselves as indies. The hybrids, authors who publish traditionally and independently at the same time. This includes popular Scottish authors such as Alanna Knight, and Lin Anderson. Finally the indie authors who have struck lucky and obtained publishing deals with a traditional publisher.

It is the latter group I am interested in for this section. I want to read some of their e-books in order to assess what attracted the publishing industry to their novels.

However, I cannot help wondering why a writer, who can

sell over 250,000 copies of their books as an indie, would want to sign with a publisher. Perhaps it is for recognition and validation of their role as an author. Or maybe they dislike the hassle of publishing their own books, because it is a fair bit of additional work, and the time could probably be better spent writing. Whatever the reason, some authors do embrace traditional publishing, and as I have explored the indie publishing scene to a great extent, it is now time to have a look at some of their books.

In 2013, James Oswald finally achieved his goal of publication by a mainstream publisher after self-publishing his crime thrillers as e-books. He was snapped up by Penguin after selling more than 50,000 copies of his first novel over the course of one month.

I chose James Oswald's first book *Natural Causes*, to read for this project, and I noticed during my research that this book was shortlisted for the CWA Debut Dagger award in 2007. However, it failed to attract a publisher and Oswald self-published *Natural Causes* in 2012.

I read the indie version of *Natural Causes*, which I had purchased prior to James Oswald being offered a contract by Penguin, therefore I am unsure how much the book will have changed after editorial input. I understand the first chapter, which I found very gruesome, has been removed and the book now commences with what was originally chapter two.

The story is interesting and well plotted with hints of the paranormal. Detective Inspector Anthony McLean, the main character, pulled me into the story and I liked him. Both the story and dialogue flowed well and were realistic, but I did find it had a slow start and it lacked suspense and pace until I had read more than half of the book. It did pick up after that and became a real page turner. However, mystery abounds throughout the book's entirety.

This is a police procedural with a paranormal element which is never too specific, being understated rather than overstated. There are some gory scenes in the book, although the most gruesome one has been removed.

Comparing it to the many indie books I have read by this stage, it was better than the reasonably good ones, but no better than some of the excellent ones. It does deserve its success, although I am sure the large amount of indie e-book sales influenced publishers in making their decision.

Despite the slow burn at the beginning of this book, this is an author I would read again.

Kerry Wilkinson has been described as one of Britain's most successful self-published authors, and in 2011 he was the top-selling author on Amazon's Kindle chart, and had sold in excess of 250,000 copies of his books. His first novel, *Locked In,* zoomed to the top of the e-book charts with both Amazon and Apple, and his later books did the same. Soon after, in February 2012, he signed a six book deal with Pan Macmillan Books.

As previously stated first books are not always the best books written by an author, but given the astronomical success of Wilkinson's first book *Locked In,* it seemed certain that this was going to be a good read. So this was the book I chose.

Perhaps my expectations were too high, but I felt the book did not quite live up to the reputation it had acquired. I tried hard to relate to Detective Sergeant Jessica Daniel, but at the end of the day I did not really care what happened to her. She did not draw me in.

This lack of connection to the character may have been something to do with the 'telling' style of the narrative where the reader is informed what is happening, rather than taking part and becoming involved in the action. I also found the explanations of every aspect of police procedure somewhat annoying, for example some of the things which had detailed explanations were – police humour, forensic testing of blood and DNA, police procedures. It is as if the author is saying that the reader is not going to understand police humour or the importance of forensic testing, so he had better put in several paragraphs explaining it.

I think the characterization also suffered because of the addition of each individual's back story as they were introduced. Many of these back stories involved minor characters and were not necessary. They had the effect of slowing the story down.

There were also some editing issues – extraneous words, wrong words used, and misspelling. Given that this was a mainstream published book (I was reading the Pan version, not the indie) I would have expected the editing to be better.

However, despite these shortcomings, the plot and storyline were good. It was a locked room mystery, although I thought it took the investigators a long time to realize how the murderer was entering and leaving the houses which were lockfast. The answer seemed obvious to me, and I am sure it will also occur to other readers. The killer's motive was less obvious giving the story a good twist with an exciting ending.

Initially I wasn't impressed with this book which had too much explanation and back story. I also felt the sex scene was a bit sudden and out of character. However, the pace picked up later and the ending was exciting.

In comparison to other indie books, I felt there were many indie authors who had published books just as good and it was not hard for me to identify indie crime books which were better. I think this flags up the way traditional publishers are identifying indie authors to contract. It is all to do with the number of downloads an indie author has achieved, and how long they stay at the top of the best-seller charts.

This novel was a good fit for the mystery and detective

category, and the police procedural, as well as the female sleuth subgenre.

Mark Edwards and Louise Voss were offered a four book deal by HarperCollins, in 2012, following the runaway success of their self-published e-books, *Killing Cupid,* and *Catch Your Death.* Both of these books had previously been rejected by traditional publishers, and it was the self-publishing sale figures which attracted their attention. According to the authors, *Killing Cupid,* was published as it was with no additional editorial input, but *Catch Your Death,* was substantially revised and edited.

However, at the end of the four book contract, HarperCollins did not renew, quoting disappointing sales, and Edwards and Voss returned to their indie origins. Once again, their indie books soared up the charts and sold in their thousands, and as Mark Edwards says *"Amazon publishing made me an offer I couldn't refuse."* The authors are now under contract to Thomas & Mercer, an Amazon imprint.

I had heard good things about *Killing Cupid,* so this was the book I chose to read. It is certainly an unusual book, not a mystery detective, but more of a psychological thriller which transports the reader deep into the minds of the two main characters.

The prologue was intriguing and definitely had the wow factor. The following chapters alternated between Alex and Siobhan, telling their story in the first person from each of their points of view, and it was fascinating. The theme was stalking, but it had unexpected twists and it was like no other stalking novel I have ever read before. And of course there were bodies, but whether it was murder or accidental death, it was hard to tell. I can't say too much about the plot for fear of giving too much away, except it was excellent. The dialogue was natural and the narrative flowed well. I enjoyed it.

Voss and Edwards are definitely writers to watch. I found it interesting that their books had more success as indies, than they apparently had with HarperCollins, or maybe the publisher's expectations were too great, or perhaps they did not provide enough marketing. I am sure that their current publishers Thomas & Mercer will be more forward looking, because Amazon certainly know how to sell books.

25
The End of the Journey

At the beginning of this book I invited you to accompany me on a journey to discover new authors who are publishing their e-books independently. The new indie breed of writer. I wanted to see if their books measured up to those published by the major publishing companies, or whether these independently published e-books were ones that should be avoided.

The task was an onerous one which took up a massive amount of my time, but I have enjoyed writing this book which has given me the opportunity to explore many subgenres of crime fiction. But more than anything else I have had the privilege of reading a variety of indie books by authors new to me. There have been good books and great books. The awful ones, not as many as I had anticipated, were discarded along the way as not worth mentioning.

In the course of writing this book I have attempted to provide information on the crime fiction genre in general, its growth over many years. The changes in writing and styles, and the newer forms as well as the not so new. I hope I have added to your knowledge of the indie world of crime fiction, as well as the growth of electronic forms of reading and the rising popularity of e-readers. I appreciate there are many people who will never forsake print books, and there was a time when I thought I was one of those. However, it is becoming ever more difficult to find places to store the many books I buy because I am a book hoarder. I do believe that if I removed all my print books from the house, the walls might cave in. So, of necessity,

I started to read e-books and was surprised at how quickly I converted to this form of reading, the bulk of which is now e-books.

This is not to say I have abandoned print books altogether. I still buy reference books and ones that take my interest which I might want to keep. And I agree there is nothing more pleasurable than holding a book, the feel of it in your hands, and the smell of it. But I invariably buy both the print and electronic versions of these books, which I then read on my e-reader, because there is nothing to beat the ease of reading in this fashion. It is also kinder on my wrists as I find it painful to hold a print book open for any length of time.

I have written this book mainly for readers, but I realise it may be of interest to writers, so I hope my section on publishing will be of help. Far be it from me to discourage any writer from following the traditional path in the search for a publisher, but do not waste too many years of your life in this pursuit, there are other ways of publishing which will help your book emerge into the world of readers.

It has been a fascinating journey, and it has been a great excuse to indulge my passion for reading. I think I must have covered most of the writing styles it is possible to write in, and among them I have read gothic, historical, and contemporary styles. The viewpoints have also varied along the way, with first person and third person being the most common, and there has even been the occasional omniscient viewpoint with an unseen narrator (usually the author). All in all, it has been a fantastic experience.

But the bonus for me, is that I have discovered some new authors I had never heard of before. Authors I will be checking regularly to see if they have produced a new e-book. I hope you will share this spin off with me because there are some genuinely good indie authors publishing e-books, who would give any traditionally published author a run for his or her money.

So, in conclusion, some of the e-books I read were good, some bad, some okay, and some were brilliant. I must say the experience has not been dissimilar to the one I would have had if I had pursued traditionally published books because I have come across some traditionally published books which were a huge disappointment. I remember leaving one behind at York railway station because it was so dreadful. So, this is a message for all you readers out there – explore the range of indie e-books, there are a lot of gems hiding away among them. No doubt there are some terrible e-books – and I came across some of them during my reading spree, although not as many as I expected – but if you use the 'Look Inside' feature of Amazon books it will help you make up your mind whether a book is worth following up.

For all you readers and writers, who have accompanied me on my journey, I have the greatest respect and appreciation, and I hope you have enjoyed it as much as I have. But now the time has come for me to take my leave. However, if you have enjoyed my company, you might like to pop over to my blog and website occasionally. I would be delighted to see you there.

Check me out at:

http://www.chrislongmuir.co.uk/

http://chrislongmuir.blogspot.co.uk/

Appendix 1

List of Sources

References – Books

Forshaw, Barry; British Crime Writing: An Encyclopedia (Vol 1 & Vol 2) 2009. Greenwood World Publishing.

Forshaw, Barry; The Rough Guide to Crime Fiction. 2007. Rough Guides.

Herbert, Rosemary, ed.; The Oxford Companion to Crime & Mystery Writing. 1999. Oxford University Press.

Keating, H.R.F.; Writing Crime Fiction. 1986. A & C Black.

Norville, Barbara; Writing the Modern Mystery. 1986. Writer's Digest Books.

Saricks, Joyce G.; The Readers' Advisory Guide to Genre Fiction. 2001. American Library Association.

References – Web sites

http://dictionary.reference.com/

http://www.merriam-webster.com/

http://medical-dictionary.thefreedictionary.com/Serial+Killer

http://uk.ask.com/ - (Ask Jeeves)

http://en.wikipedia.org/wiki/Main_Page

http://www.britannica.com/

http://www.gutenberg.org/

http://edition.cnn.com/

http://www.fbi.gov/

http://edinburghebookfestival2014.wordpress.com/about/

http://www.slideshare.net/nebraskaccess/history-of-e-books-ereaders

Reports

http://authorearnings.com/the-report/

https://kdp.amazon.com/help?topicId=A3OG0G04TL5KMG
(Kindle Million Club)

Blogs

http://www.thepassivevoice.com/12/2013/why-i-turned-down-a-three-book-new-york-print-deal-to-self-publish/

http://www.thecreativepenn.com/2011/12/09/self-publishing-indie-author-definition/

http://www.carolebarrowman.com/the-dark-threads-of-tartan-noi/

http://hunterswritings.com/2012/10/05/mysteries-vs-thrillers-vs-crime-fiction/ - (Mysteries vs Thrillers vs Crime Fiction)

http://www.shotsmag.co.uk/feature_view.aspx?FEATURE_ID= 120 – (The Strange Appeal of Crime Fiction by Andrew Taylor)

http://www.deanwesleysmith.com/?page_id=860 - (Killing the Sacred Cows)

http://jakonrath.blogspot.co.uk/2010/12/you-should-self-publish.html - (Newbies Guide to Publishing)

http://www.deanwesleysmith.com/

http://davidgaughran.wordpress.com/

http://historicalcrime.com/ - (B.D. Logue)

http://marshrachel.wordpress.com/

http://laurasheehan.wordpress.com/

http://deesavoy.com/

http://roxannestclaire.com/blog/

http://www.christopherfowler.co.uk/blog/

Appendix 2

About Chris Longmuir

Chris Longmuir is a well known Scottish writer, and if you listen to her You Tube trailers where she reads the first chapters of her books, in a distinctive Scottish accent, you could be forgiven for thinking she was born and bred in Scotland. But appearances can be deceptive, because Chris was born in Wiltshire in the south of England. Admittedly, she fled England at the tender age of two, but this does not give her the excuse to masquerade as a Scot, no matter how much she would like to.

She was a solitary child, painfully shy, and lived most of her childhood within the pages of books. At one stage she even attempted to read her way through the local library. Needless to say she failed because she had only one lifetime to live. But immersing herself into the imaginary world of books allowed her to escape from the nitty gritty of daily life and playground bullies. She made up stories in her head and lived imaginary adventures, but these were never committed to paper because of her belief that she did not have the skill to do this.

Life trundled on. She worked in various jobs and was a shop assistant, office worker, factory worker, and a bus conductress. It was only later that she gained a university degree and became a social worker. But before that happened she got married and lived a comparatively normal life with a doting husband and children, although she didn't quite manage the usual two point five kids.

In the meantime, she continued to devour books, and developed an itch to write them. Once she started writing, Chris never stopped. She started to sell short stories and articles, and was happy with that for a time. But that damned itch came back to goad her into writing a novel. So, that's what she did.

Chris wrote several novels before her first one was published. It was the usual round of submission and rejection. But along the way she started winning awards, culminating in the biggie – the Dundee International Book Prize, which led to immediate publication. The rest, as they say, is history.

Since then, Chris has published three books in her Dundee Crime Series, one book in a new historical crime series – the Kirsty Campbell novels – and one historical saga. And, of course, this non-fiction book. She has been traditionally published but is now an indie, and proud of it.

Chris has now found her forte in crime writing and is never happier than when she is killing off her characters. In fact, her friends joke that she cannot write a shopping list without adding a murder or two. But they also say that she is a very nice lady – honestly, she really is.

Chris continues to scratch her writing itch, and is currently writing a new historical crime novel, although there are many more stories rolling around in her head. It's the same problem she met when she decided to read her way through the library – she only has one lifetime!

Check Chris out at:

http://www.chrislongmuir.co.uk/

http://chrislongmuir.blogspot.co.uk/

Also by Chris Longmuir

DUNDEE CRIME SERIES

Night Watcher
Dead Wood
Missing Believed Dead

KIRSTY CAMPBELL NOVELS

The Death Game

HISTORICAL SAGAS

A Salt Splashed Cradle

SHORT STORIES

Ghost Train & Other Stories
Obsession & Other Stories

NON-FICTION

Crime Fiction and the Indie Contribution

www.ingramcontent.com/pod-product-compliance
Lightning Source LLC
Chambersburg PA
CBHW060626290526
45793CB00001B/156